THE ART OF MAKING GOOD CANDIES AT HOME

The Art of Making Good Candies at Home

MARTIN K. HERRMANN

photographs by JOHN M. HERRMANN

Doubleday & Company, Inc., Garden City, New York

ISBN: 0-385-06030-0
Library of Congress Catalog Card Number 66-20924
Copyright © 1966 by Martin K. Herrmann

9

Preface

The best way to use this book is to treat it as a course in candy making. Read the sections on sugar boiling, chocolate tempering, and chocolate dipping very thoroughly. Assemble all raw materials and working tools, and then make each kind of candy or one of each group at least once, starting with the first recipe, and continuing through the book. The recipes are arranged in such a manner as to start you off with simple candies involving only sugar boiling and handling. Then the recipes get more elaborate, building on the experience you gained by making the previous ones, until you will finally be experienced enough to make the last ones in the book, and also to dip candies in chocolate or bonbon coating.

After you have gone through the book as a course, it will be easy for you to make any kind of candy in it later on. Also, you may occasionally wish to refer to the Glossary in the back of the book for a quick review of the various methods and procedures you have learned. The Glossary also discusses a few types of candy which do not appear in this book and explains why they do not.

Contents

Preface   **7**

Chapter 1 – Getting Started   **17**

    The History of Candy Making   **17**

    Raw Materials Needed for Candy Making   **20**

    Tools, Utensils, and Other Materials Needed for
    Candy Making   **21**

    General Instructions for Sugar Boiling and Candy
    Making   **22**

Chapter 2 – Hard Candies   **25**

    General Procedure for Making Hard Candies   **25**

    Butterscotch Drops   **29**

    Mint Drops or Small Bars   **29**

    Lemon Squares   **30**

    Cinnamon Drops   **30**

    Strawberry or Raspberry Squares or Oblongs   **30**

    Licorice Drops   **31**

    Lollipops   **31**

Pulled Molasses Taffy   32

Molasses Mint Taffy   36

After-Dinner Mints   36

Peanut Brittle   37

Cashew Brittle   40

Coconut Brittle   40

Filbert Brittle   41

Brazil Brittle   41

Chapter 3 – Caramel   42

Milk Caramel   42

Chocolate-Nut Caramel   45

Turtles   46

Chapter 4 – Chocolate and Bonbon Coating   48

Chocolate Melting and Tempering   48

Chocolate Dipping   52

Bonbon Coating   58

*Chapter 5 – Chocolate Bark, Clusters,
and Dipped Nuts*   59

Preparing the Nuts for Dipping   59

Chocolate Bark   60

Chocolate-Nut Clusters   60

Chocolate-Dipped Nuts   61

Chapter 6 – Marshmallow   62

Toasted Marshmallow   62

Rocky Road   66

Chapter 7 – Fondant   70

Basic Sugar Crème   70

Procedure for Making Hand-Rolled Crème
   Centers for Chocolate Dipping   75

Fruit and Mint Crème Centers   78

Thin-Mint Crème Centers   78

Mint Crème Leaf Centers   78

Orange Crème Centers   79

Lemon Crème Centers   79

Strawberry or Raspberry Crème Centers   80

Coconut Crème Centers   80

Summer Mint and Fruit Crème Patties   81

Summer Mint Patties   82

Lemon Patties   83

Orange Patties   83

Raspberry Patties   83

Chapter 8 – Buttercrème   84

    Basic Buttercrème   84

    Procedure for Making Buttercrème Centers   86

    Rum-Nut Crème Centers   87

    Chocolate Crème Centers   87

    Chocolate-Mint Crème Centers   88

    Buttermint Crème Centers   88

    Opera Crèmes   89

    Maple-Walnut Crème Centers   90

    Vanilla Fudge   90

    Chocolate Fudge   92

    Penuche Fudge and Penuche Chocolate Bars   92

Chapter 9 – Quickie Candies   94

    Basic Batch   94

    Rum-Walnut Candies   95

    Coffee Doughnuts   95

    Cherry Crèmes   96

    Opera Crèmes   96

    Coconut Balls   97

    Peanut Butter Squares   97

    Nutty Goody   98

    Mint Patties   98

Chocolate White-Dots 98

Neapolitans 99

Chapter 10 – Marzipan 101

Pure Almond Paste 101

Chocolate-Coated Marzipan Pieces 101

Marzipan Confect 103

Marzipan Potatoes 105

Summary 106

Chapter 11 – Fruit and Mint Jellies,
   Made with Agar-agar 107

Basic Agar Jelly Batch 107

Neapolitan Jellies 108

Sugar-Sanded Jellies 109

Chocolate-Coated Jellies 109

Mint Jellies 109

Lemon Jellies 110

Strawberry Jellies 110

Grape Jellies 110

Orange Jellies 111

Raspberry Jellies 111

Chapter 12 – Fruit and Mint Jellies,
   Made with Gelatine and Applesauce 112

Basic Applesauce Jelly 112

Sugar-Sanded Jellies 113

Chocolate-Coated Jellies 113

Apple-Nut Jellies 113

Cinnamon-Apple Jellies 114

Lemon Jellies 114

Mint Jellies 114

Orange Jellies 115

Raspberry Jellies 115

Sandwich Jelly, Green and White 115

Sandwich Jelly, Red and White 116

Strawberry Jellies 117

Chapter 13 – Specialties 118

Tender Honey Nougat 118

Chocolate Nougat 121

Almond Toffee 122

Divinity 126

Buttered Caramel Popcorn 127

French Whipped-Cream Truffles 129

Coconut Mounds 132

Salt-Water Taffy 133

Pecan Rolls 135

Candied Fruit Peel 138

Praline 140

Chapter 14 – Cordials   143

   Note   143

   Alcoholic Fruit Cordials   143

   Non-Alcoholic Cordials   150

Glossary   154

*Appendix A: Some Sources for Candy Flavorings,
   Colors, and Other Raw Materials*   161

*Appendix B: Some Sources for Tools, Utensils,
   and Other Materials for Candy Making*   164

Index   167

Recipes for items printed in *italics* may be located
by consulting the Index.

CHAPTER *1*

Getting Started

THE HISTORY OF CANDY MAKING

The art of candy making is quite old, dating from times when ancient peoples discovered the sweetest nectar on earth—honey. Chocolate, and the boost it gave to the art of candy making, dates from the discovery of how to turn cocoa beans into a concoction called "chocolatl"—the Food of the Gods.

The first descriptions of candylike sweets come from Europe, about 600 years before the birth of Christ. At that time, sweetmeats in the shops of Rome already played a great part in the splendor of that city, though only the wealthy people could afford them.

Starting in 1470, some of the confections were made in Germany. German gingerbread bakers were well known for their cakes and other sweets, as well as for their gingerbread, although in those days "sweets" meant something quite different from what we know by that name today. Most of these early sweets consisted of a sticky, sugary concoction, made from dried fruit, nut meats, sesame or poppy seeds, and spices, mixed and held together with honey. They were cut into pieces, and rolled in flour, chopped nut meats, and poppy or sesame seeds to keep them from sticking together.

Beginning in the sixteenth century, large, luxurious banquets became the vogue at the courts of the emperors and kings of Europe. The efforts of these royal men to outdo each other led to the exploitation of the art and trade of these early confectioners, and thereafter this food was almost completely reserved for the nobility. It remained so for a long time.

Honey was the only sweetening used in these early confections, until the discovery of America and subsequent explorations brought sugar to the Old World in the sixteenth century. America was also responsible for two other important advances in the confectionery industry. The more important of these was cocoa. It was first tasted by Cortez in 1519, when the Aztec emperor Montezuma served a royal drink called "chocolatl" to the conquering Spaniards. It was thought of by the Indians as a food of the gods. The Spaniards did not like the bitter taste of the drink, however, and so they added sugar to it. When introduced to Spain, the drink was very well liked, and as in the New World, it was reserved for the aristocracy. The drink also underwent several changes; its flavor was improved by the addition of cinnamon, and it was served hot. The other contribution of the New World, vanilla, was also used to improve the flavor.

During the seventeenth century, while the gingerbread bakers were still producing "sweets," people in monasteries and apothecaries also began producing them and selling them to the public, but they were also very diligent in developing and selling other confections, closer to what we know as candy, using the newly introduced vanilla, sugar, and some cocoa, though they had not yet found a way to make chocolate. The commercial confectioner's trade probably dates from these monasteries and apothecaries of the seventeenth century.

Late in the seventeenth century, confectioners, who were employed by grocers who had the right to bake cakes and produce sweets for sale to the public, resumed the bulk of the commercial trade, first as a sideline, along with gingerbread and sweetmeats, until the demand for the candylike sweets grew so much that some of them began to specialize in just producing sweets and candies. These confectioners were called "conditors."

Many people had tried and failed, but a method of producing chocolate for eating was finally developed in 1876 by Daniel Peter in Switzerland. No one knows just when people started coating sweets with chocolate, but when they did, the popularity of candies became so great that the confectionery industry was swept off its feet, and began to grow and spread faster and faster, to keep up with the demand.

Since then, the candy making and confectionery industry has spread all over the civilized world. Today it is one of the world's largest industries. In the United States alone, over three billion pounds of candies and chocolates are produced yearly, for an average consumption of about eighteen pounds of candy per capita.

RAW MATERIALS NEEDED FOR CANDY MAKING
(in the approximate order of their use)

Granulated white sugar
Brown sugar
Clear Karo syrup
Butter or margarine
Lecithin (optional)
Crisco or a similar product
   for greasing baking sheets
Salt
Candy flavors
Paste food colors (preferable to
   liquid food colors)
Finely granulated citric acid
Light molasses
Raw and toasted nut meats
   (unsalted)
Baking soda
Shredded coconut, white and
   toasted
Evaporated milk
Unsweetened chocolate (also
   called chocolate liquor)
Milk and bittersweet chocolate
   coating
White or colored bonbon
   coating

Chocolate and colored
   decorettes
Raisins and candied fruit
Knox unflavored gelatine
Flour
Fresh and canned fruits
Strawberry and raspberry jams
Marshmallow topping
Confectioners' powdered sugar
Sweetened condensed milk
Instant coffee
Cocoa powder
Peanut butter
Pure almond paste
Agar-agar
Dried or fresh egg whites
Honey
Popcorn
Whipping cream
Dry yeast
Brandy, rum, or other hard
   liquors (optional)

Raw materials you may not be able to obtain readily from your local grocer's shelf are discussed in the back of the book, in Appendix A.

TOOLS, UTENSILS, AND OTHER MATERIALS
NEEDED FOR CANDY MAKING

A good candy thermometer. This is most important. It should be very accurate, with a range between 100° F. and 310° F. I prefer the Taylor Candy-Jelly-Frosting thermometer. It costs about $3.50. DO NOT buy or use a dial-type or oven thermometer. These are not accurate enough for candy making.

Flat wooden stirring paddles, same as or similar to those used for stirring paint.

Small, clean brush. A basting brush will do.

Steel spatula with a stiff blade, about 3–3½ inches long and 3–3½ inches wide at the bottom, that will not bend easily.

Small- and medium-sized pots and a double boiler.

Baking sheets, with and without borders, baking pan (about 8×12×2 inches), bread loaf pan, and beating bowls.

Measuring cup and spoons.

Chocolate dipping fork.

Cherry dipping fork.

Electric egg beater.

Household scale (optional). Should be graduated in ¼-ounce fractions, capacity 1½–2 pounds.

Cotton or leather gloves, but not the fuzzy type.

Wax paper, brown wrapping paper, locker wrap (freezer paper), and aluminum foil.

Chocolate crinkle-cups.

Grooved rubber mat.

Cheese grater.

Lollipop sticks.

Tools and utensils you may not be able to obtain readily from local hardware, five-and-ten, or variety stores are discussed in the back of the book in Appendix B.

GENERAL INSTRUCTIONS FOR
SUGAR BOILING AND CANDY MAKING

Before you start to make any candy batch it is important that you have all the necessary tools ready, all ingredients including water weighed or measured and ready to use, all colors and flavors ready, and the baking sheet or pan prepared for the batch to be poured on for cooling. Baking sheets and pans are used dry, moistened with water, greased, or lined with paper or foil, depending on what the recipe calls for to accommodate the finished batch. The information on how the baking sheet or pan should be prepared is marked with an asterisk (*) in every recipe. You should also read the recipe through completely before starting to make the candy.

To make sure that the cooking temperatures given in the recipes are correct, deduct 1° F. from the given temperatures for every 500 feet of elevation; or else, check your thermometer in boiling water. If it reads 212° F., cook all the recipes to the temperatures given. If it shows a higher or lower temperature reading than 212° F., adjust the cooking temperatures accordingly. It is a good idea to check your thermometer in boiling water anyway, no matter where you live, because cooking temperatures, and therefore thermometer accuracy, are very important.

Use a small pot, about 5–5½ inches wide and 4–5 inches high. Because most batches are small, the bulb of the thermometer would not be completely submerged in a wider pot, where the batch would be shallower. Always make sure that the thermometer bulb is completely submerged and that it does not touch the bottom or side of the pot.

If the quantity of an ingredient, either wet or dry, is given

GETTING STARTED

23

in cups or fractions thereof, it should be measured in a
measuring cup. One cup = 8 fluid ounces. If the quantity
is given in ounces (oz.), the ingredient should be weighed
out on a scale. Use measuring spoons as and where indicated.
The finished weight of the candy batches described in this
book ranges from 9 ounces to 1½ pounds. If larger batches
are desired, you may double or triple the amounts of all the
ingredients without fear of spoiling the batch. You may have
to work a little harder on some of the candies, but if the
multiple weights and measures of all the ingredients are
correct and you follow the procedure carefully and use
common sense, you will not fail.

Always keep a small pot or deep dish of cold water handy
near the stove for the paddle, thermometer, and water brush.
These small batches demand constant attention, and if you
have to leave the stove for several minutes to rinse something
in the sink while the batch is on the fire, it may stick, overcook, or even spoil. If you have to leave the stove for some
reason, take the batch from the fire while you are away.

Only when all the above preparations are completed should
you put the ingredients in the pot and on the stove—in exact
sequence, as described in each individual recipe.

For perfect results, the sugar must dissolve completely,
and no undissolved sugar crystals should be left on the side
of the pot. When the mixture of sugar and carefully measured
water and other liquids is dissolved and has boiled up for
the first time, wash down the sugar crystals adhering to the
side of the pot, while batch keeps boiling, using a small,
clean brush dipped lightly in cold water, in order to dissolve
them. Or else, put a cover on the pot for 3 minutes, during
which the resulting steam will dissolve the sugar crystals.
Also wash the adhering sugar crystals down from the stirring
paddle. Try not to use too much water for doing this, just a

Washing down adhering sugar crystals   *Sugar boiling*

fairly wet brush, or the covered method which does not require any additional water.

The thermometer is put into the batch only when the batch has boiled up for the first time, the sides of the pot and the stirring paddle are washed down, and all the ingredients which have to be cooked to a certain degree are in the pot.

When the batch has reached the correct temperature, according to the recipe, take the batch from the fire at once; otherwise it will keep cooking and may get too hard or too dark or may spoil altogether. Then stir in any other ingredients called for in the recipe, and continue as the recipe indicates.

If you feel that the consistency of a batch is not quite correct, cooking it 2–3 degrees lower than indicated in the recipe will make the finished product softer; cooking it 2–3 degrees higher than indicated in the recipe will make it firmer and drier.

CHAPTER 2

Hard Candies

GENERAL PROCEDURE FOR MAKING HARD CANDIES

Put carefully measured sugar, water, and Karo syrup into a pot, put it on the stove at medium heat, and stir. When the batch has boiled up for the first time, wash the sugar crystals down from the side of the pot and the stirring paddle, add the butter or margarine, if it is called for, put the thermometer in the pot, and cook without further stirring to the temperature given in the recipe. Then take the pot from the fire and add any indicated salt, coloring, or flavoring and stir in gently, except in the case of those hard candies made with citric acid. Citric acid does not stand high temperatures, and therefore has to be folded into the batch after it has been poured onto the baking sheet and has cooled down for about 2 minutes. Sprinkle the acid over the whole surface of the batch, and when the batch is folded together, flatten it out to about ¼ inch thick and score it in the usual manner. The batch would, of course, be too firm for making round drops at this stage, and reheating would destroy the citric acid and make the candies sticky.

To make candy drops, drop small round patties about the size of a quarter onto a greased baking sheet with a tea-

Making hard candy drops

spoon. If the candy in the pot gets too firm for spooning, reheat it gently until soft enough and continue spooning.

If square pieces are wanted, pour the whole batch onto a greased baking sheet without borders. Do not disturb it for at least 2 minutes. Then sprinkle on the citric acid, if called for, and fold the borders of the circular batch over into the center to form a square mass. Flatten it out by pressing a slightly greased hand or spatula on top. Loosen the batch from the baking sheet with a spatula or knife and turn it over. This cools the batch evenly, without hard edges. While the batch is still soft and plastic, score the surface by pressing the greased edge of a knife or long spatula on the surface of the batch in parallel lines 1 inch apart. Then turn the sheet a quarter turn and repeat the scoring in the same manner,

Pouring the hard candy batch for other shapes

Folding in the edges of the batch

Spreading the batch

Scoring the batch for hard candy squares

Scored hard candy batch and finished drops

forming 1-inch squares. Other shapes and designs can also be made, using the shapes suggested by the names of the hard candies and your own imagination. Cookie cutters can also be used for this.

Cool the drops or scored batch completely by placing the sheet near an open window or in a cool room, but not in the refrigerator or the pieces will stick. Soon the drops will be firm and will come off the sheet easily. Break the batch into pieces if it has been scored.

Pieces should be wrapped individually in waxed paper or cellophane or foil to prevent sticking. If you do not want to wrap them individually, they may be "sanded" (sugar-coated). To sand pieces, dip a clean kitchen towel in cold water and wring it out until it is just damp. Spread the moist towel out on a table and place the pieces on one half of the towel. Make sure that no piece is on top of another. Then fold the other half of the towel over the pieces and wipe the towel with your hand to moisten the pieces in between. They should get sticky all over, but not wet. Open the towel and put the pieces, 10–15 at a time, into a plate or wide, low bowl filled with granulated sugar. Roll and move them around in the sugar until they are evenly coated, and then take them out. If there are any bare spots on the pieces, they were not completely or sufficiently moistened before being put into the sanding dish. Continue until all of the pieces are sanded. Sugar-sanded pieces will not stick and can be kept in a cellophane bag or covered container for a long time.

BUTTERSCOTCH DROPS

> 1 cup white sugar
> ¼ cup brown sugar
> ¼ cup water
> ¼ cup Karo syrup
> 1 tablespoon butter or margarine
> ½ teaspoon salt
> ¼ teaspoon butterscotch flavor
> *Greased baking sheet without borders

Cook to 290° F. Follow general procedure *Hard Candies*.

MINT DROPS OR SMALL BARS

> 1 cup white sugar
> ¼ cup water
> ¼ cup Karo syrup
> A few drops peppermint oil
> Light green food color or paste
> *Greased baking sheet without borders

Cook to 290° F. Follow general procedure *Hard Candies*.

LEMON SQUARES

  1 cup white sugar
  ¼ cup water
  ¼ cup Karo syrup
  A few drops lemon flavor
  Light yellow food color or paste
  ¼ teaspoon citric acid
  *Greased baking sheet without borders

Cook to 290° F. Follow general procedure *Hard Candies*, being sure to fold the citric acid in after the batch has been poured on the sheet and cooled for about 2 minutes.

CINNAMON DROPS

  1 cup white sugar
  ¼ cup water
  ¼ cup Karo syrup
  A few drops cinnamon flavor
  Light red food color or paste
  *Greased baking sheet without borders

Cook to 290° F. Follow general procedure *Hard Candies*.

STRAWBERRY OR RASPBERRY SQUARES OR OBLONGS

  1 cup white sugar
  ¼ cup water
  ¼ cup Karo syrup

¼ teaspoon strawberry or raspberry flavor
Dark red food color or paste
¼ teaspoon citric acid
*Greased baking sheet without borders

Cook to 290° F. Follow general procedure *Hard Candies*, being sure to fold the citric acid in after the batch has been poured on the sheet and cooled for about 2 minutes.

LICORICE DROPS

>1 cup white sugar
>¼ cup brown sugar
>¼ cup water
>¼ cup Karo syrup
>¼ teaspoon anise flavor
>1 tablespoon black color paste
>*Greased baking sheet without borders

Cook to 290° F. Follow general procedure *Hard Candies*.

LOLLIPOPS

Lollipops of any size can be easily made by dropping the hard candy drops on the ends of lollipop sticks, placed on a greased baking sheet. Also, Halloween lollipops can be made by decorating the pieces, while still hot and soft, with small, colorful candy drops and kernel corn, pressed into the candy, for eyes, nose, and mouth or teeth. Some suggestions for lollipop colors and flavors:

Yellow	lemon flavor, but without citric acid
Green	mint or vanilla
Red	cinnamon
Orange	orange flavor, but without citric acid

PULLED MOLASSES TAFFY

    1 cup white sugar
    ½ cup light molasses
    ½ cup Karo syrup
    ½ teaspoon salt
    ¼ teaspoon butterscotch flavor
    *Greased baking sheet without borders

Put the sugar, molasses, and Karo syrup into a higher pot than usual; the molasses will cause the batch to boil quite high. Place on the stove at low heat and stir until the sugar is dissolved. Wash the sugar crystals down from the pot and stirring paddle. Take out the stirring paddle and cook on medium heat to 294° F., stirring gently with the thermometer. Then take the pot from the fire and stir in the salt and flavor. Let stand for 5 minutes for precooling, and then pour the batch onto the greased baking sheet.

Pouring out the molasses taffy batch

After a few minutes, fold the edges of the batch into the center to form a square mass. Move the batch to a cooler spot on the baking sheet, turn it over, and fold in the edges again. Repeat three or four times. This cools the batch evenly.

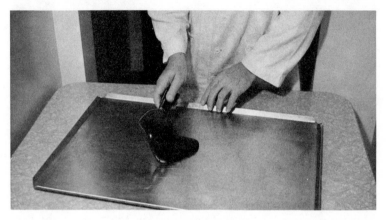

Cooling the batch

When the batch is cool enough to handle, but still soft and plastic, form a rope 2 inches thick. Using buttered fingers or clean gloves, pull the rope until it is 2–3 feet long and

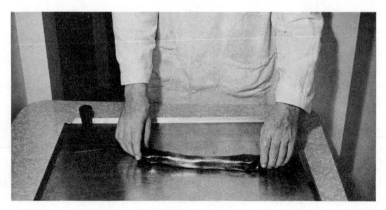

Forming a rope

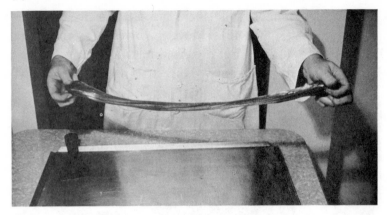

Pulling the rope

fold in half. Twist the rope and repeat. Continue doing so until the candy is light in color. This will take about 6–8 minutes of pulling. Finally, stretch it into a rope ½ inch thick on a clean table and score lines on the surface about 1 inch apart. Cool the rope and break it at the score lines; wrap the pieces individually in cellophane, or sand them with sugar.

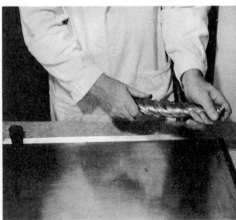

Folding the rope   *Twisting the rope*

Pulling the rope again

Scoring

The finished pulled molasses taffy

MOLASSES MINT TAFFY

    1 cup white sugar
    ½ cup light molasses
    ½ cup Karo syrup
    ¼ teaspoon salt
    ¼ teaspoon peppermint oil
    *Greased baking sheet without borders

Cook to 294° F. Follow the procedure for *Pulled Molasses Taffy.*

AFTER-DINNER MINTS

    2 cups white sugar
    ½ cup water
    ¼ cup Karo syrup
    8 drops peppermint oil
    *Greased baking sheet without borders
    *Baking sheet without borders, sprinkled with powdered
      sugar

Put the sugar, water, and Karo syrup into a pot and stir together. Put the pot on the stove at medium heat and keep stirring. When the batch boils up for the first time, wash the sugar crystals down from the sides of the pot and the stirring paddle. Put in the thermometer, and cook to 260° F. without further stirring. Take the pot from the stove and let stand 2 minutes, to precool the batch, then gently stir in the peppermint oil. Pour the batch onto the greased baking sheet.

    After a few minutes, fold the edges of the batch into the center to form a square mass. Move the batch to a cooler spot on the baking sheet, turn it over, and fold in the edges again. This cools the batch evenly.

When the batch is cool enough to handle, but still warm and plastic, form a rope 2 inches thick. Using buttered fingers or clean gloves, pull the rope until it is 2–3 feet long and fold in half. Then twist the rope and repeat. Continue doing so until the candy is light in color. This will take about 6–8 minutes of pulling. Finally, stretch it into a rope ½ inch thick on a clean table. Cut the rope into ½-inch-long pieces with a pair of scissors, and put them, side by side, on the baking sheet sprinkled with powdered sugar. Sprinkle powdered sugar on top of the cut mints and set aside overnight in a warm room, to soften the centers. Next day, brush or sift off the excess powdered sugar. Store the mints in a cellophane bag or covered jar.

PEANUT BRITTLE

(Made with fresh, raw peanuts. This gives the best flavor)

1 cup white sugar
¼ cup water
¼ cup Karo syrup
2 tablespoons butter or margarine
½–¾ cup raw, shelled Spanish peanuts
½ teaspoon salt
¼ teaspoon baking soda
A few drops vanilla flavor
*Greased baking sheet

Put the sugar, water, and Karo syrup into a pot and on the stove at medium heat. When it boils up for the first time, wash the sugar crystals down from the side of the pot and the stirring paddle. Stir in the butter or margarine. Cook to 260° F. without further stirring. Then stir in the peanuts and continue stirring gently with the thermometer. Cook to 310° F., take from the stove, and stir in the salt, baking soda, and vanilla flavor.

Cooling the peanut brittle batch

Pour the batch onto the greased baking sheet and spread it out. Wait a few minutes for it to cool slightly. Then loosen it from the sheet with a long knife, turn it over, and stretch it out as thin as possible. Let the batch cool at room temper-

Stretching

ature until it is hard and brittle. Break it apart. To keep it from sticking, store it in a closed jar or tin, or in a closed cellophane bag that will keep moisture out.

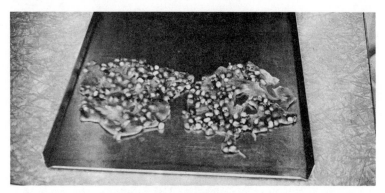

The finished peanut brittle

(Made with roasted, salted peanuts)

½–¾ cup roasted, salted Spanish peanuts, preferably dry-roasted
1 cup white sugar
¼ cup water
¼ cup Karo syrup
2 tablespoons butter or margarine
¼ teaspoon baking soda
A few drops vanilla flavor
*Greased baking sheet

Place the peanuts in a frying pan and heat slightly. Set aside, but keep warm. Put the sugar, water, and Karo syrup into a pot and place it on the stove at medium heat. When it boils up for the first time, wash the sugar crystals down from the side of the pot and the stirring paddle. Stir in the butter or margarine. Then cook to 310° F., stirring gently with the thermometer, and take the pot from the heat. Stir in the warmed peanuts, baking soda, and vanilla flavor. Pour the batch onto the greased baking sheet and continue as above.

CASHEW BRITTLE

> 1 cup white sugar
> ¼ cup water
> ¼ cup Karo syrup
> 2 tablespoons butter or margarine
> ½–¾ cup cashews, halves and pieces (raw, or roasted and salted)
> ½ teaspoon salt (omit if salted cashews are used)
> ¼ teaspoon baking soda
> ¼ teaspoon orange flavor (Yes! It enhances the flavor)
> *Greased baking sheet

Follow the procedure for either *Peanut Brittle* made with raw peanuts, or *Peanut Brittle* made with roasted, salted peanuts, depending on the type of cashews you are using.

COCONUT BRITTLE

> 1 cup white sugar
> ¼ cup water
> ¼ cup Karo syrup
> 2 tablespoons butter or margarine
> ½ cup shredded white coconut
> ¼ teaspoon salt
> ¼ teaspoon baking soda
> ¼ teaspoon coconut flavor
> *Greased baking sheet

Follow the procedure for *Peanut Brittle* made with raw peanuts.

FILBERT BRITTLE

1 cup white sugar
¼ cup water
¼ cup Karo syrup
2 tablespoons butter or margarine
½–¾ cup raw filberts, whole or pieces
½ teaspoon salt
¼ teaspoon baking soda
¼ teaspoon vanilla flavor
*Greased baking sheet

Follow the procedure for *Peanut Brittle* made with raw peanuts.

BRAZIL BRITTLE

1 cup white sugar
¼ cup water
¼ cup Karo syrup
2 tablespoons butter or margarine
½–¾ cup chopped raw Brazil nuts
½ teaspoon salt
¼ teaspoon baking soda
¼ teaspoon butterscotch flavor
*Greased baking sheet

Follow the procedure for *Peanut Brittle* made with raw peanuts.

CHAPTER 3

Caramel

MILK CARAMEL

   ¾ cup white sugar
   2 tablespoons water
   1 cup Karo syrup
   4 tablespoons (½ stick) butter or margarine
   ¾ cup evaporated milk
   ½ teaspoon salt
   A few drops vanilla flavor
   *Well greased baking sheet with borders

Put the sugar, water, and Karo syrup into a pot and on the stove at medium heat and stir. Wash the sugar crystals down from the side of the pot and the stirring paddle when the batch boils up for the first time. Stir in the butter or

Cooking the caramel batch and adding the milk

margarine. When the batch starts boiling again, add the evaporated milk very slowly,. a little at a time, stirring constantly. Stir the caramel vigorously, touching all points of the bottom and sides of the pot every few seconds. This is to prevent the milk from scorching. It should take about 5 minutes for all the milk to be added to the batch. Continue boiling and stirring for another 10–12 minutes and take the batch from the fire.

TESTING THE BATCH: Put a quart-sized saucepan in the sink and fill it with cold water. Keep the water running in a steady, small stream, into the pan and out into the sink and drain. It is important that the water keeps running at a constant temperature. Take a little bit of the caramel out of

Testing the caramel in cold water

Forming a ball

Testing ball for firmness

the pot with a teaspoon and submerge it in the cold water. After a few seconds, take the caramel off the spoon and try to roll it into a ball, keeping it submerged in the cold water. If it readily forms a ball and feels fairly firm, but not too hard, exactly as a finished piece of caramel should feel when cold, the batch is ready. This is called the *medium ball* stage of boiling.

If the caramel does not form a ball or feels too soft, as it probably will the first time you test it, put the batch back on the stove, heating and stirring thoroughly, for a few minutes. Then repeat the test and continue heating and testing until the batch is ready. If, for some reason, the batch has cooked too long, and the test shows a ball that is too firm, or even hard, simply add about 2 tablespoons of hot water to the batch, stir, boil up again, and test as before, until the caramel shows the right consistency, a fairly firm ball, in the cold water.

When the batch is ready, leave it off the stove after the test and stir in the salt and flavor. Pour the batch onto the well-greased baking sheet, spreading it about ½ inch thick. Put it into the refrigerator. Let it cool until firm. Then take it out of the tray and cut it into strips about ¾ inch wide.

Cutting the finished caramel batch

Use a long knife, cutting back and forth swiftly in a sawing motion. That way, it will cut easily and will not stick. Cut the strips into squares and wrap them individually in foil or waxed paper to prevent sticking, or else dip them in chocolate.

If the cooled caramel should not come out of the tray easily, reheat the bottom of the tray gently by holding it over a low flame on the stove for a moment. The caramel will come off the tray readily then. Turn the batch and lay it on a cutting board or baking sheet without borders and sprinkle both sides lightly with flour. If the caramel is not firm enough for cutting, put it back into the refrigerator until it is firm.

CHOCOLATE-NUT CARAMEL

¾ cup white sugar
2 tablespoons water
1 cup Karo syrup
4 tablespoons (½ stick) butter or margarine
¾ cup evaporated milk
1½ squares unsweetened chocolate (chocolate liquor)—
   more if desired
¼ teaspoon salt
¼ teaspoon rum flavor
A few drops vanilla flavor
⅓ cup chopped walnuts or toasted almonds
*Well greased baking sheet with borders

Follow the procedure for *Milk Caramel,* cooking the chocolate-nut caramel to the *medium ball* stage. Add the unmelted chocolate liquor when all the milk is in; it will melt and mix in readily while you stir the boiling caramel. Stir the chopped nuts into the finished, cooked batch at the same time the salt and flavor are added.

TURTLES

¾ cup white sugar
2 tablespoons water
1 cup Karo syrup
4 tablespoons (½ stick) butter or margarine
¾ cup evaporated milk
½ teaspoon salt
A few drops vanilla flavor
3–4 cups chopped pecan or walnut meats
Tempered chocolate
*Baking sheet with borders

Make one batch of *Milk Caramel*, but cook only to the *soft ball* stage (the caramel should form a soft ball when tested under cold water). Add the salt and flavor when it is ready, and leave it in the pot to cool slightly.

Spread as many of the nuts as possible on the baking sheet with borders, quite densely and not less than ½ inch thick. Pour small amounts of caramel onto the nuts with a teaspoon. Do not make these drops of caramel much larger than a quarter, or the finished turtles will be too large, and do not

Making turtles; dropping hot caramel on the pecans

set them too close to each other, or the caramel will run together. If the caramel in the pot gets too stiff for spooning, stir and reheat it gently. When the caramel on the nuts has cooled, lift the turtle centers out with your dipping fork and set them aside, caramel side up. Push the nuts together and add more if necessary, to make an even surface, and spoon more caramel onto the nuts. Repeat this procedure until all the caramel is used up. Some of the nuts will be left over, but the total amount is needed to work with. Dip the turtle centers in tempered chocolate, so that the finished pieces will have the caramel on the bottom.

Turtles ready for dipping

One batch of caramel will make 8–9 dozen turtle centers. If you do not wish to use the whole caramel batch for turtles, put the pot with the remaining caramel back onto the stove at medium heat. Stir constantly and cook the batch to the *medium ball* stage, but be careful not to overcook. It will take only a few minutes to reach the *medium ball* stage. Then pour the caramel onto a well-greased baking sheet with borders and proceed as with milk caramel.

CHAPTER *4*

Chocolate and Bonbon Coating

CHOCOLATE MELTING AND TEMPERING

Correct tempering and handling of chocolate is a fine art. To master it completely, as is especially necessary for commercial purposes, requires a thorough knowledge of its physical properties, and its reactions to melting, cooling, and handling. I have found, however, while teaching candy making to hundreds of people in thirty-hour adult education courses, that very good results can be obtained by following a few basic steps as given here for preparing chocolate for candy dipping.

Have at least several pounds of chocolate coating on hand, so that there will always be enough to work with. For the sake of economy, it is recommended that you buy "break-up" chocolate (broken up slabs of chocolate coating), usually available in large pieces or in pound bags. Better yet, and most economical, are the ten-pound slabs of commercial chocolate coating used by candy plants, and often available through them. Any chocolate coating can be remelted and used over again until it is all used up. Store the chocolate in a cool, dry place, but not in the refrigerator.

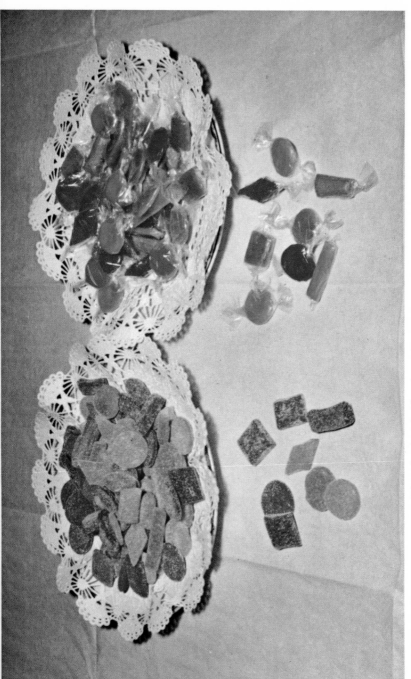

Plate 1   Sanded hard candies and wrapped hard candies

Melt chocolate only in a double boiler. First put hot water from the kitchen tap into the bottom pot of the double boiler, enough to cover the bottom and sides of the upper pot. The water should never be hotter than 140° F. This is very important, because chocolate, especially milk chocolate, will coagulate (form grainy lumps) at temperatures over 140° F. Cut about 2 pounds of chocolate coating into small pieces and put them into the upper part of the double boiler. After 10 or 15 minutes, when part of the chocolate has melted, stir it with a dry spoon or stirring paddle. Stir again from time to time, until all the chocolate has melted. Always work in a cool room (65–68° F.) or near an open window when working with chocolate.

While the chocolate is melting, grate about ¼ pound of chocolate into fine particles on a cheese grater. For best results, do this in a cool room, using cold, hard chocolate of the same type as the melting chocolate. The chocolate dust should be as fine as sawdust, so sift it through a kitchen sieve or strainer if necessary, removing the larger particles. This chocolate dust is called "seeding" chocolate. It should be stored in a cool, dry place.

From the double boiler pour about two-thirds of the chocolate, which should now be completely melted, into a clean, dry baking sheet with low borders. *Be sure* to wipe the bottom of the upper pot of the double boiler before pouring out the chocolate! Even one or two drops of water in the chocolate will make it thick and may even make it impossible for dipping. Put the upper pot, with the balance of the melted chocolate, back into the lower pot of the double boiler to keep it warm.

Spread the melted chocolate out on the baking sheet with a dry, clean steel spatula to precool it to 85–90° F. Move the chocolate coating around on the tray with short, quick motions of the spatula, from the sides to the center and back out again. Continue doing so. From time to time, put a dab of chocolate on your wrist or lower lip. When it feels neither warm nor cool, its temperature is correct, and it should not be worked any more.

Chocolate tempering; seeding with grated chocolate

Now sprinkle 1 heaping teaspoonful of the chocolate dust on the surface of the precooled chocolate and mix in thoroughly with the spatula. This will "seed" the chocolate

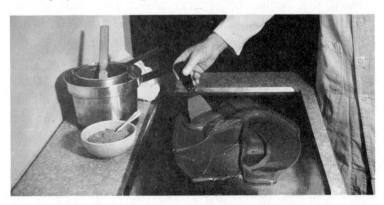

Mixing in the seeding and finishing the tempering

coating with unmelted cocoa butter crystals (contained in the chocolate dust) and will help the chocolate to set up properly on the dipped candies. Seeding the chocolate with the cold dust and mixing the dust in will further cool the precooled (90° F.) batch to about 80° F. or slightly lower. Check the temperature on your wrist or lower lip again; it should feel cool. The chocolate is now ready for dipping.

Because, as mentioned before, chocolate dipping should be done in a cool room, the tempered chocolate on the tray will keep on cooling and may soon get too thick for further dipping. When you notice that the chocolate is getting too thick for further dipping, add a little warm chocolate from the double boiler and mix it in thoroughly with the spatula. Be careful not to add too much warm chocolate at a time. Add just enough to make it workable, and recheck the temperature. It should feel cool on the lower lip or wrist. An exact estimate of how much warm chocolate to add cannot be given here, because this depends on the temperature of the melted chocolate in the double boiler and the temperature and amount of the chocolate on the tray.

If you mix too much warm chocolate into the dipping batch and the chocolate feels warm on your wrist or lip, sprinkle some more seeding chocolate on the surface and mix it in thoroughly. Test the temperature again. If it is still too warm, add a little more cold seeding chocolate, until the temperature of the dipping chocolate is again correct.

Since the chocolate does cool, you should keep an adequate supply of melted chocolate ready in the double boiler. Adjust the temperature of the water in the double boiler to about 110° F. by adding hot or cold tap water to hold the chocolate at this temperature for adding to the dipping batch as needed to warm it, and also to replace chocolate used on the dipped pieces.

If the dipping chocolate on the tray becomes too cold and there is no more warm chocolate left to adjust the temperature, the best thing to do is to scrape all the chocolate from the tray back into the double boiler and start over again.

Always be sure to check the temperature of the dipping chocolate before continuing dipping. This is very important. A sign of well-tempered chocolate is that after 20 or 30 pieces have been dipped, the first pieces start to set up. They should set up with a fine, satinlike sheen. That is, if you are working in a cool room (65–68° F.), as mentioned before. If the room you are working in is warmer than 70° F., dip only twenty to thirty pieces at a time and let them set near an open window or at some place cool enough to set them. You may use the refrigerator to cool the pieces, but leave them in it only until they are well set, which should take less than ½ hour. If you leave chocolates in the refrigerator too long, they will sweat and lose their sheen when brought back to room temperature.

CHOCOLATE DIPPING

Chocolate dipping of candies has been done by hand for many years, both in this country and abroad. Professional hand dipping is done literally by hand. The dipper uses only her hand to cover the pieces of candy with chocolate, strip off the surplus chocolate, set it down on dipping or wax paper, and decorate the top of the piece with her fingers.

Apart from the fact that many people do not much like to have their hands deep in chocolate, dipping chocolate candies this way demands a great deal of skill and cannot be learned in a few easy lessons. Therefore, another method, the use of a dipping fork, is described here. It is used mainly in Europe, and it has been used with great success and has proved itself in the many candy classes I have taught over the past years.

Cover the table on which you plan to dip the candies with several layers of newspaper. Then put a clean kitchen towel on top. This will keep the tray with the tempered chocolate from losing heat too fast, holding the temperature of the chocolate more constant. Put the centers to be dipped on a baking sheet without borders on your left. Place the tray with the tempered chocolate in front of you in the center of the table. Raise the back of the tray with a wax paper box or other long box. NOTE: The best thing to do is to use the tray with low borders on which you tempered the chocolate. If you wish, though, the tempered chocolate can be put into a small pot or saucepan. In this case, fill the pot almost to the brim. Place a baking sheet without borders on the right side of the table, next to the dipping tray, and cover it with wax paper.

If you use the baking sheet with low borders for the chocolate, gather the chocolate together in the front of the

Setup for chocolate dipping

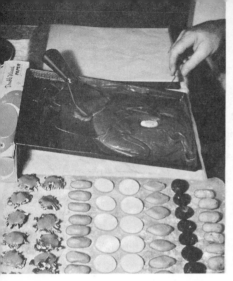

Putting a center into the chocolate, bottom up

Covering the bottom of the center with chocolate

tray, as near to you as possible. The deeper the chocolate, and the closer to the rim of the tray, at the front where you will work, the easier it is to dip the candies.

With your left hand place one candy center, upside down in the chocolate, deep enough that two-thirds of the piece is submerged in the coating. Hold the dipping fork, relaxed

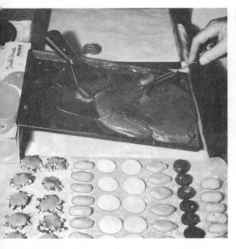

Lifting the coated center out of the chocolate

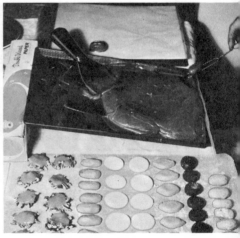

Wiping off surplus chocolate

and not too tightly, in your right hand. Dip the fork lightly into the coating a few inches from the right side of the candy piece, holding the fork flat, with the prongs side by side. Move the fork, with the chocolate gathered between the prongs, over the candy, coating it completely. Then move the fork (still held flat) back over the bottom of the piece (which is on top) to wipe off surplus chocolate. This regulates the thickness of the coating on the future bottom of the piece.

Now place the prongs of the fork under the piece and lift it up out of the dipping chocolate. Then lower it back onto the surface of the chocolate 2 or 3 times, touching the surface of the chocolate with the fork and candy only lightly each time. This pulls surplus chocolate from the sides of the piece. Move the fork with the dipped piece over the spot on the wax paper where you want to place it. Flip the piece over by turning the fork between your thumb and index finger, placing the piece right side up on the wax paper.

Setting the piece on the paper, right side up, and decorating it with lines

Decorate the piece by touching the top lightly with the prongs of the fork, lifting the fork about ⅛ inch above the piece, but staying in contact with the chocolate, and then pulling the fork away from the piece, along the lines of the

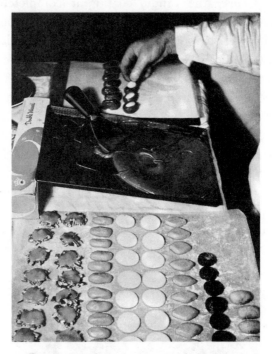

Decorating dipped pieces with blanched almond halves

prongs and still ⅛ inch above the piece. Decorations can be varied by using only one prong for a single line or using both prongs of the fork twice, making four lines, or criss-crossing the lines or using the points of the prongs to get a scrambled effect. You can also sprinkle chocolate decorettes or colored decorettes on the dipped pieces, or lay blanched almond halves or walnuts on top, while the chocolate is still soft. If you do not wish to have any decor on top of the piece, as on thin mints, place the piece in the dipping chocolate right-side-up, and place it on the paper with the fork beneath it. Then pull the fork gently out from under the piece.

Setting down thin mints   *No decor*

Make sure that there is not too much chocolate on the piece before setting it down. If the chocolate runs down on the paper and forms a flat ring around the base of the piece, either you did not strip off enough coating from the bottom and sides of the piece, as described above, or the chocolate is too warm and there is not enough seeding chocolate in it. Correct this right away, before dipping too many pieces! As mentioned before, for best results, dipping should be done in a cool room (65–68° F.) If this is not possible, follow the directions for cooling the dipped pieces, as outlined in the section on chocolate tempering.

Finished dipped centers, L. to R. caramels, tender honey nougat, turtles, rum-nut crèmes, chocolate crèmes, mint crème leaves (note leaf-vein decor), thin mints, strawberry crèmes

BONBON COATING

Bonbon coatings are made from sugar, milk, hydrogenated coconut oil, flavors, and colors. They come in white, yellow, pink, and green. Because their melting points are higher than that of chocolate, these coatings are used mainly for summer confections. They are also used, of course, when pastel colors are desired on candies.

Bonbon coatings do not have to be tempered for dipping. Just cut the coating into small pieces and melt them in a double boiler, as is done with chocolate. Then cool the coating down to about 96° F. and start dipping. The candies will set up quickly, even at room temperature, and will have a nice, satiny sheen.

White bonbon coating can be colored, but only with oil-soluble food colors. Or else, a little cocoa powder can be mixed into the melted white coating to give it a light brown coloring. Never mix bonbon coating with chocolate, though, because such a combination causes nothing but trouble. It will seldom set up firmly, even when tempered, and it will tend to disintegrate later.

CHAPTER 5

Chocolate Bark, Clusters, and Dipped Nuts

PREPARING THE NUTS FOR DIPPING

The nut meats called for in all the recipes in this chapter should be unsalted. Nuts such as peanuts, cashews, almonds, and filberts should be toasted. If you cannot buy these toasted nut meats unsalted, buy raw nut meats and toast them yourself, as described in the Glossary. If you do so, be sure to let them cool completely before using them, or else the chocolate will not set up properly, or will turn gray. Nuts such as Brazils, walnuts, and pecans, of course, should not be toasted.

The nuts used in *Chocolate Bark* should be chopped into fairly small pieces, so that the bark can be spread as thinly as possible. Large nuts, such as walnuts, pecans, and Brazils, for use in *Chocolate-Nut Clusters* should be chopped into smaller pieces, and smaller nuts, such as almonds, cashews, filberts, and peanuts, need not be chopped. For individual *Chocolate-Dipped Nuts*, only large nut meats, such as walnut and pecan halves and Brazil nuts, should be used, and of course, should not be chopped at all.

CHOCOLATE BARK

> 1 cup melted, tempered chocolate
> ¼ cup chopped walnuts (see above)
> ¼ cup chopped, toasted almonds
> 2 tablespoons raisins
> *Baking sheet on which you tempered the chocolate,
>   and another baking sheet, covered with wax paper

Stir the chopped nuts and the raisins into the melted and tempered chocolate, on the baking sheet which you used to temper the chocolate. Spread the batch fairly thinly on the wax paper and cool it until firm. Break the finished bark into fairly large pieces and store it in a cellophane bag or other closed container, in a cool place.

Chocolate bark, of course, can be made in many ways, with or without raisins, and with many kinds of nuts. It can also be made with bonbon coating, as a summer candy.

CHOCOLATE-NUT CLUSTERS

> 1 cup nut meats (see Preparing the Nuts for Dipping)
> 1 cup melted, tempered chocolate
> *Baking sheet on which you tempered the chocolate,
>   plus another baking sheet, covered with wax paper

Add the nuts to the tempered chocolate on the baking sheet and mix them together. Then spoon out clusters of nuts onto the baking sheet covered with wax paper, using two tablespoons. Let them set in a cool room or in the refrigerator until firm. Again, as with bark, chocolate-nut clusters can be made with a great variety of nuts or raisins, and can also be made with bonbon coating.

CHOCOLATE-DIPPED NUTS

Large nut meats
Tempered chocolate
*Baking sheet covered with wax paper

Dip the nut meats in the tempered chocolate, using the regular dipping fork. Set them on the baking sheet covered with wax paper. If you wish, you can also dip the nuts again, once the first coating of chocolate has set, in order to make the pieces larger. You can also dip the chocolate in two different types of chocolate coating or bonbon coating, or both, but MAKE SURE that if you want a chocolate-bonbon piece, you dip it in the bonbon coating *first*. If you do it the other way around, the higher-melting-point bonbon coating will melt the chocolate already on the piece, they will mix, and neither coating will set up properly. Also make sure that the first coating on the nut is set up well before dipping it again.

CHAPTER 6

Marshmallow

TOASTED MARSHMALLOW

⅓ cup cold water
2 pkgs. Knox unflavored gelatine (=½ oz.)
1¼ cups white sugar
⅓ cup water, additional
1 cup Karo syrup
½–1 teaspoon vanilla flavor
½ teaspoon toasted coconut flavor
2½ cups toasted, shredded coconut
*Baking pan (about 8×12×2 inches) lined
   with brown paper

Put ⅓ cup of cold water into a cup and pour the gelatin into
the cup. Stir until all of the gelatine is wet, but no longer.
Set aside.

Put the sugar and the rest of the water into a pot. Boil up
once, to dissolve the sugar. Wash down the side of the pot
and boil up once more. Then take the pot from the fire and
pour the sugar syrup into a beating bowl. Add the Karo syrup
and then the soaked gelatine and dissolve it completely in
the syrup. Beat with an electric beater at medium speed, until
the batch holds a good peak. This will take about 20 minutes.

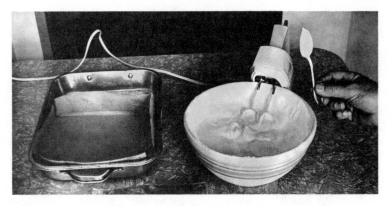

Making marshmallow, checking the peak

Stir in the flavors and pour the batch into the paper-lined pan, spreading it about 1¼ inches thick. Cover the surface of the batch with toasted coconut and let it set 1 or 2 hours or overnight in a cool place. Then take the batch out of the pan,

Pouring the marshmallow into a paper-lined pan

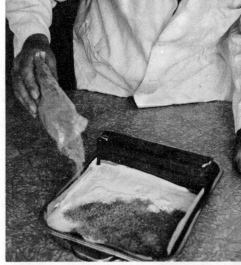

Sprinkling toasted coconut on top of the marshmallow for toasted marshmallows

Dipping the knife in water to prevent sticking   *Cutting*

with the paper still on it, and cut it into 1-inch squares with a long knife. Dip the knife in cold water frequently to prevent sticking. Then turn the batch over and soften the paper, which should still be in one piece, with a wet cloth. Let it soak a minute or two and peel the paper off. Pick the pieces

Peeling off the paper   *Separating the marshmall*

rshmallow

Moistening the paper for removal

apart and roll them in the remaining coconut, lightly brushing off any excess coconut. This can be saved for use with the next batch. To keep the marshmallow fresh and tender, store the pieces in a cellophane bag or closed jar after they have dried for about 2 hours at room temperature.

ces; rolling them in coconut

Finished toasted marshmallow pieces

ROCKY ROAD

⅓ cup cold water
2 pkgs. Knox unflavored gelatine
1¼ cups white sugar
⅓ cup water, additional
1 cup Karo syrup
½ teaspoon vanilla flavor
Some flour
3 cups milk chocolate
½ cup chopped walnuts
*Baking pan (about 8×12×2 inches) lined with brown paper
*Same pan, later lined with wax paper or foil

Make one batch of *Toasted Marshmallow* as above, omitting the coconut flavor and the toasted coconut. Cover the batch with flour when it is in the paper-lined pan, instead of with coconut, and also roll the pieces in flour instead of in coconut. Remember to brush off the excess flour. Let pieces dry at room temperature for several hours, or overnight.

Separating the cut marshmallow and rolling the pieces in flour

Removing the excess flour

Preparing the chocolate

Melt and temper all the chocolate. Because the marshmallow is usually quite cool, though, the tempered chocolate has to be rewarmed slightly before stirring in the marshmallow pieces and nuts. This is done by holding the tray with the tempered chocolate about a foot above a low flame on the stove for a few moments, until the bottom of the tray feels warm. Stir the chocolate again. Then stir the marshmallow pieces and chopped walnuts gently into the chocolate,

Mixing in the marshmallow

Adding the nuts

while it is still on the tempering tray. When the marshmallow
and nuts have been stirred into the chocolate, pour the batch
into the baking pan lined with wax paper or foil and spread
it about 1½ inches thick. Let it cool, and wrap the finished
batch in foil or polyethylene, and cut off only what you wish

Blending

Rocky road ready for cooling

to eat soon. This will keep the rest of the batch fresh and tender for weeks.

If the chocolate gets too firm, or even sets up, before all the marshmallow is in, it was too cold. If necessary, rewarm it again, as described above, and continue mixing. If the finished Rocky Road should look streaky, the chocolate was too warm or was not stirred and blended well enough or did not have enough seeding.

CHAPTER *7*

Fondant

BASIC SUGAR CRÈME

(For making fruit or mint crèmes or for use in recipes calling
for fondant as an ingredient)

> 2 cups white sugar
> ½ cup water
> 2 tablespoons Karo syrup
> *Large baking sheet, moistened lightly with water just
>   before the batch is poured on

Put the sugar, water, and Karo syrup into a pot and on the
stove at medium heat and stir. When the batch boils up for
the first time, wash the sugar crystals down from the sides
of the pot and the stirring paddle. Put the thermometer in
and cook to 242° F. without further stirring. Then pour the
batch out onto the baking sheet, which should be moistened
lightly with water by wiping it with a clean, moist cloth just
before the batch is poured on. Do NOT scrape the batch out
of the pot, or it may grain. Let the batch cool on the sheet,
moving the sheet to a cooler spot on the table from time to
time. This gives more even cooling of the batch. After about
3 minutes, touch the batch lightly with greased fingertips

Pouring the cooked batch on the tray

to check the temperature. The batch should just feel warm, not hot. If it feels hot, let it cool some more, until it is just warm. Then it is ready for creaming.

To cream the batch, scrape it together in the center of the baking sheet with a stiff spatula (with a blade 3–3½ inches wide at the bottom and about as long) and then spread it out over the whole sheet, using long, firm strokes. Hold the spatula firmly and almost flat, spreading the batch about ¼ inch thick. Then gather the whole batch together and spread

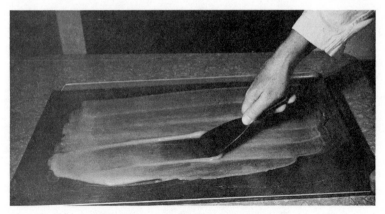

Starting to cream the fondant; will look this way after 2–3 minutes

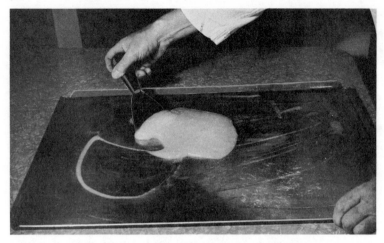

Scraping together into center periodically

it out again. Continue doing so until the batch gets more and more opaque, and finally sets up firm and white. Creaming the batch will take about 10–15 minutes, depending on how the batch is worked. The more pressure that is applied to the spatula (friction), the sooner the batch will set up. If the batch has not set up after 15 minutes of creaming, put the

Spreading out again; will look this way
after about 5 minutes of continuous creaming

Fondant getting whiter and firmer as creaming is continued

sheet, with the batch spread out on it, on the stove, over one burner at very low heat. Keep moving the batch around on the sheet with the spatula while rewarming. Feel the bottom of the sheet and the batch; when it feels warm, remove it from the heat and continue creaming. The batch will soon set up.

If you have a marble slab, you can, of course, use it for creaming fondant, because a marble slab is so much heavier than a baking sheet, and therefore will not slide around on the table while creaming. MAKE SURE, though, that the batch does not get too cold before starting the creaming (do not wait longer than 5 minutes; start as soon as it is just warm), as it is not practical to put the marble slab, with the batch on it, on the stove for reheating, in case it does not set up within 15 minutes. In this case, you will just have to continue creaming, until the batch sets up, without reheating it. And the next time, start creaming the batch a little earlier and warmer when using the marble slab. Moisten the slab before pouring on the batch, just as if you were using a baking sheet.

Fondant has set up

When the batch has set up, scrape it from the sheet and knead it by hand until it gets smooth and a little softer. If there are any hard lumps in the batch, take them out, crush them, and knead them separately, until they are as soft as the rest of the batch. Knead the batch only enough to make it hold together and feel smooth. Otherwise, it may become too soft. If the fondant is to be used later, let the finished

Kneading it by hand, to smooth out

batch cool at room temperature for a few hours, then wrap it in foil and store it in a cool place. Otherwise, proceed at once making crème centers, while the fondant is still warm.

Finished fondant

You can, of course, eat fondant as is, but it will taste quite bland without additional flavors. Crème centers can also be eaten uncoated, but again will not taste quite right, because the amounts and types of flavors take into account the flavor of the chocolate in which the centers are to be dipped.

PROCEDURE FOR MAKING HAND-ROLLED CRÈME CENTERS FOR CHOCOLATE DIPPING

Warm the fondant to about 120° F. by spreading it out on a baking sheet and putting it on the stove over one burner at very low heat. When the bottom of the sheet feels warm, turn the fondant over and heat in the same manner. Knead the fondant together on the center of the sheet, spread it out again, and reheat. Repeat the procedure until the fondant is evenly heated. The fondant should be soft, but it should not flow. If freshly made fondant is used, slight reheating is necessary only if there is no more heat left in the batch.

Put the sheet with the warmed fondant on the table and work in all the other ingredients the recipe calls for, until the batch is evenly colored. If necessary, adjust the amounts of color and flavor to give good taste and color that is not too strong. Try not to knead the batch too much, or it may get too soft to handle.

If the batch should get too soft to form good centers for dipping, it may be because it is too warm. In this case, let it cool at room temperature for about an hour, until it is only lukewarm and firm enough to form centers. If the softness is caused by lengthy storage, or if the batch is still too soft after being cooled, you can also knead in a small amount, 1–2 tablespoons, of powdered sugar to make the batch firmer, but only if absolutely necessary. Powdered sugar added to the fondant at this stage will tend to make it slightly coarse.

Next, sprinkle powdered sugar onto a clean table or baking sheet and roll the batch into a long, even rope not more

Shaping crème centers

Shaping crème centers

than 1 inch in diameter. Slice the rope into pieces about ½–¾ inch long. Sprinkle powdered sugar onto your hands and shape the pieces for variety, making round, square, triangular, oblong, or oval, etc., pieces to suit your taste. Suggestions are given in each recipe. For best results, make sure that the bottoms of the pieces are not quite as wide as the sides or the tops of the pieces. This will help prevent large chocolate bottoms when the pieces are dipped. Let the crème centers set on the sheet in a dry and fairly cool place, but not in the refrigerator, for several hours or overnight. When the centers are set, dip them in chocolate.

If you like very soft crèmes, dissolve ¼ teaspoon of dry yeast in ½ teaspoon of water and add it to the batch along with the flavor and color. After the centers have been dipped in chocolate, the yeast will soften them considerably in one or two weeks, and it will keep them soft for many weeks thereafter.

FRUIT AND MINT CRÈME CENTERS

Each of these recipes is based on one batch of *Fondant*, about 1 pound, 2 ounces. If you wish to use one batch of fondant for two or more kinds of crème centers, just divide the fondant batch and the amounts of the other ingredients by two, three, or four, etc. Shape the flavored and colored fondant into a rope, cut it into slices, and shape these appropriately, according to what they contain. Suggestions are given in each recipe. Put the finished centers onto a baking sheet covered with wax paper and sprinkled with powdered sugar and let them set well, preferably overnight, before dipping them in milk or bittersweet chocolate or in bonbon coating. Remember to add the dissolved yeast, as described in the procedure section, if you like softer crèmes.

THIN-MINT CRÈME CENTERS

To 1 batch of *Fondant* add:

¼ teaspoon peppermint oil (more or less, to suit taste)

Shape these centers into round, flat patties about the size of a half-dollar, but not thicker than ¼ inch. When they are dipped, do not put any decor on top.

MINT CRÈME LEAF CENTERS

To 1 batch of *Fondant* add:

¼ teaspoon peppermint oil (more or less, to suit taste)
A few drops green food color

Roll the pieces into the shape of a football. Then press them flat on wax paper to about ¼ inch thickness, into the shape of a leaf. You can also put decor in the shape of leaf veins on top, when you dip the mint crème leaves.

ORANGE CRÈME CENTERS

To 1 batch of *Fondant* add:

> Rind of ½ orange, finely chopped
> A few drops orange oil
> 10–12 drops lemon juice or ¼ teaspoon citric acid, dry
> A few drops orange food color

Shape into round, flat pieces ½ inch thick.

LEMON CRÈME CENTERS

To 1 batch of *Fondant* add:

> Rind of ½ lemon, finely chopped
> A few drops lemon oil
> 10–12 drops lemon juice or ¼ teaspoon citric acid, dry
> A few drops yellow food color

Shape into round, flat pieces ½ inch thick.

STRAWBERRY OR RASPBERRY CRÈME CENTERS

To 1 batch of *Fondant* add:

> ¼ cup recooked jam
> ¼ cup powdered sugar, sifted
> 6 drops lemon juice
> A few drops red or pink food color

Strawberry or raspberry jam, as bought from the grocery shelf, contains too much moisture, for making good candy centers. It has to be recooked first. Put about ½ cup of the jam into a small pot, place it on *low* heat, and stir continuously. Cook the jam for 10–15 minutes. Then take the pot from the fire and put it into a shallow pan filled with cold water, stirring the jam occasionally, to cool it. The powdered sugar is added to the centers to help compensate for the moisture in the jam. This powdered sugar will not cause coarseness, because it will be inverted by the natural fruit acid in the jam.

COCONUT CRÈME CENTERS

To 1 batch of *Fondant* add:

> ½ cup finely shredded white coconut
> ¼ cup marshmallow topping
> A few drops coconut flavor

Shape into flat, oval pieces about ½ inch thick.

Plate 2   Assorted chocolate-dipped candies. Help yourself!

SUMMER MINT AND FRUIT CRÈME PATTIES

Each of these recipes is based on one batch of *Fondant*, about 1 pound, 2 ounces, made one or several days before. If you wish to make more than one kind of patties, just divide the fondant batch and the other ingredients by two, three, or four.

To make the patties, cut the fondant into small pieces and put them into a double boiler on low heat. Add the additional Karo syrup, color, and flavor, and stir thoroughly. Heat the fondant to 150–160° F., but not higher, or else the finished patties will form white spots later. Do not heat any lower than 150° F., either, or else the patties will not set up.

With a teaspoon, drop small amounts of the batch onto a baking sheet lined with wax paper, or onto a rubber mat with parallel grooves about ⅛ inch apart (wetted well under running cold water before the patties are dropped on) to form small, round patties. In a few minutes, the patties will be firm and can be taken off the baking sheet or rubber mat.

Dropping summer mint and fruit crème patties on grooved rubber mat

If the batch gets too firm while spooning, stir and reheat it to 150–160° F. again in the double boiler. If it is still too firm, add a few drops of Karo syrup while reheating. Let the patties dry overnight, and then store them in a closed jar or cellophane bag. These patties should not be coated.

Finished fruit and mint crème patties

SUMMER MINT PATTIES

1 batch *Fondant*

> 2 tablespoons Karo syrup
> ¼ teaspoon peppermint oil (more or less, to suit taste)
> A few drops green food color (optional)
> *Baking sheet lined with wax paper, or grooved rubber mat moistened with cold water

LEMON PATTIES

1 batch *Fondant*

    2 tablespoons Karo syrup
    ½ teaspoon lemon oil
    10–12 drops lemon juice
    A few drops yellow food color
    *Baking sheet lined with wax paper, or grooved rubber
      mat moistened with cold water

ORANGE PATTIES

1 batch *Fondant*

    2 tablespoons Karo syrup
    ½ teaspoon orange oil
    10–12 drops lemon juice
    A few drops orange food color
    *Baking sheet lined with wax paper, or grooved rubber
      mat moistened with cold water

RASPBERRY PATTIES

1 batch *Fondant*

    2 tablespoons Karo syrup
    ½ teaspoon raspberry flavor
    10–12 drops pink food color
    *Baking sheet lined with wax paper, or grooved rubber
      mat moistened with cold water

CHAPTER 8

Buttercrème

BASIC BUTTERCRÈME

 1½ cups white sugar
 ¼ cup brown sugar
 2 tablespoons water
 ⅓ cup Karo syrup
 2 tablespoons butter or margarine
 ½ cup evaporated milk
 *Large baking sheet, moistened lightly with water just
    before the batch is poured on

Put the sugar, water, and Karo syrup into a pot and on the
stove at medium heat and stir. When the batch boils up for
the first time, wash the sugar crystals down from the sides
of the pot and the stirring paddle, and add the butter or
margarine. When the batch boils up again, start adding the
evaporated milk, a little at a time. Keep the batch boiling and
stir vigorously. Add the milk very slowly. It should take 3–4
minutes for all the milk to be added. When all the milk is in,
put in the thermometer. Keep stirring as much as is possible
with the stirring paddle, or else take the paddle out and stir
the batch carefully with the thermometer. Cook the batch
to 240° F. Then pour it out onto the baking sheet, which

should be moistened lightly with water by wiping it with a clean, moist cloth just before the batch is poured on. Let the batch cool on the sheet, moving the sheet to a cooler spot on the table from time to time. This gives more even cooling of the batch. After about 3 minutes, touch the batch lightly with greased fingertips to check the temperature. The batch should feel just warm, not hot. If it feels hot, let it cool some more, until it is just warm. Then it is ready for creaming.

To cream the batch, scrape it together into the center of the sheet with a stiff steel spatula (with a blade about 3–3½ inches wide at the bottom and about as long) and then spread it out over the whole sheet, using long, firm strokes. Hold the spatula firmly and almost flat, spreading the batch about ¼ inch thick. Then gather the whole batch together and spread it out again. Continue doing so until the batch gets more and more opaque, and finally sets up firmly. Creaming the batch will take about 10–15 minutes, depending on how the batch is worked. The more pressure is applied on the spatula (friction), the sooner the batch will set up.

If the batch has not set up after 15 minutes of creaming, put the sheet, with the batch spread out on it, on the stove over one burner at very low heat. Keep moving the batch around the sheet with the spatula while rewarming. Feel the bottom of the sheet and the batch; when it feels warm again, remove it from the heat and continue creaming. The batch will soon set up.

If you have a marble slab, you can use it for creaming buttercrème also, but again, be sure to start creaming it as soon as the batch feels just warm, because it cannot be reheated. If the batch has not set up within 15 minutes, you will just have to continue creaming until it does, and next time start a little sooner when you use the marble slab.

Moisten the slab before you pour on the batch, just as if you were using a baking sheet.

When the batch has set up, scrape it off the sheet and knead it by hand until it gets smooth and a little softer. If there are any hard lumps in the batch, take them out and crush them, and knead them separately, until they are as soft as the rest of the batch. Knead the batch only long enough to make it hold together and make it feel smooth. Otherwise, it may become too soft. If the buttercrème is to be used later, let the finished batch cool at room temperature for a few hours, then wrap it in foil and store it in a cool place. Otherwise, proceed at once making crème centers, while the buttercrème is still warm. You can, of course, eat the buttercrème as is, but as with fondant, it will taste quite bland. The undipped crème centers can also be eaten, but they will not taste quite right, either, because the flavor of the chocolate is missing.

PROCEDURE FOR MAKING BUTTERCRÈME CENTERS

Each of these recipes, except the buttermint, opera, and maple walnut crème centers, is based on one batch of basic *Buttercrème*, about 1 pound, 6 ounces. The buttermint, opera, and maple walnut crème centers are based on buttercrème recipes containing different amounts of white and brown sugar. However, if you wish to use one batch of *Basic Buttercrème* for two or more kinds of crème centers, no matter what kind they are, divide the finished batch into two, three, or four, etc. parts and add only ½, ⅓, ¼, etc. of the color, flavor, and other ingredients given for whole batches. Make sure that the centers are well set, preferably overnight, in a cool, dry place, but not in the refrigerator, before dipping them in chocolate.

If you like very soft crème centers, dissolve ¼ teaspoon of yeast in ½ teaspoon of water and add it to the batch along with the flavor and color. After the centers have been dipped in chocolate, the yeast will soften them considerably in one to two weeks, and it will keep them soft for many weeks thereafter.

*Baking sheet sprinkled with powdered sugar to dry the centers on (for each of the following recipes).

RUM-NUT CRÈME CENTERS

Knead into 1 batch of *Basic Buttercrème:*

- ¼ teaspoon salt
- ½ teaspoon rum flavor or 2 teaspoons rum
- ¼ cup chopped walnuts

Shape into square or rectangular pieces, about ½ inch thick. When the centers have set firm enough to handle, dip them in milk or bittersweet chocolate.

CHOCOLATE CRÈME CENTERS

Knead into 1 batch of *Basic Buttercrème:*

- ¼ cup unsweetened chocolate (also called chocolate liquor; melt before adding)
- ¼ teaspoon salt
- ¼ teaspoon rum flavor

Shape into round or oval pieces, about ½ inch thick. When the centers have set firm enough to handle, dip them in milk or bittersweet chocolate. Decorate the pieces with half of a blanched almond on top of each.

Making rum-nut and chocolate crème centers

CHOCOLATE-MINT CRÈME CENTERS

Knead into 1 batch of *Basic Buttercrème:*

> ¼ cup unsweetened chocolate (also called chocolate liquor; melt before adding)
> ½ teaspoon salt
> ¼ teaspoon peppermint oil

Shape into round, flat pieces about ½ inch thick. When the centers have set firm enough to handle, dip them in milk or bittersweet chocolate.

BUTTERMINT CRÈME CENTERS

Make 1 batch of *Basic Buttercrème,* but use:

    1¾ cups white sugar
    2 tablespoons water
    ⅓ cup Karo syrup
    2 tablespoons butter or margarine
    ½ cup evaporated milk

Knead in:

    ¼ teaspoon salt
    ¼ teaspoon peppermint oil (more or less, as desired)

Shape into round patties, about the size of a half-dollar and ¼ inch thick. When the centers have set firm enough to handle, dip them in milk or bittersweet chocolate.

OPERA CRÈMES

Make 1 batch of *Basic Buttercrème,* but use:

    1¾ cups white sugar
    2 tablespoons water
    ⅓ cup Karo syrup
    2 tablespoons butter or margarine
    ½ cup evaporated milk

Knead in:

    ¼ teaspoon salt
    1 teaspoon vanilla flavor

Roll into ball-shaped pieces, about ¾ inch in diameter. When the centers have set firm enough to handle, dip them in bittersweet chocolate.

MAPLE-WALNUT CRÈME CENTERS

Make 1 batch of *Basic Buttercrème,* but use:

1¾ cups brown sugar
2 tablespoons water
¼ cup Karo syrup
2 tablespoons butter or margarine
½ cup evaporated milk

Knead in:

¼ teaspoon salt
1 teaspoon maple flavor or ½ teaspoon vanilla flavor
⅓ cup chopped walnuts

Shape into square or triangular pieces about ½ inch thick. When the centers have set firm enough to handle, dip them in milk or bittersweet chocolate.

VANILLA FUDGE

1½ cups white sugar
¼ cup brown sugar
2 tablespoons water
⅓ cup Karo syrup
2 tablespoons butter or margarine
½ cup evaporated milk
¼ cup marshmallow topping
½ cup chopped walnuts or toasted almonds
½ teaspoon salt
¼ teaspoon vanilla flavor

*Large baking sheet for creaming the batch, lightly
moistened with water just before the batch is poured
on
*Baking pan, about 8×12×2 inches, lined with lightly
greased wax paper

Put the sugar, water, and Karo syrup into a pot and on the
stove at medium heat and stir. When the batch boils up for
the first time, wash the sugar crystals down from the sides of
the pot and the stirring paddle, and add the butter or margarine. When the batch boils up again, start adding the evaporated milk, a little at a time. Keep the batch boiling and
stir vigorously. Add the milk very slowly. It should take
3–4 minutes for all the milk to be added. When all the milk
is in, put in the thermometer. Keep stirring as much as
possible with the stirring paddle, or else take the paddle out
and stir the batch carefully with the thermometer. Cook the
batch to 240° F. Then pour it out onto the baking sheet,
which should be moistened lightly with water by wiping it
with a clean, moist cloth just before the batch is poured on.

Let the batch cool on the sheet until it is just warm, moving
it to a cooler spot on the table from time to time, and testing
the temperature with lightly greased fingertips. Then cream
the batch as is described in the recipe for *Basic Buttercrème*,
but when it starts getting opaque and dull, shortly before setting up, add the marshmallow topping. Cream the batch
1–2 minutes longer and mix in the chopped nuts, salt, and
flavor. Spread the batch about ¾ inch thick in the wax paper-lined baking pan. Roughen the surface of the fudge by
drawing the tip of a small spatula or palette knife over the
surface in a criss-cross motion. Let the fudge cool and set
completely. Then take it out of the pan, cut it into squares,
and wrap them in wax paper or foil, or keep them in a closed
jar or tin.

CHOCOLATE FUDGE

1½ cups white sugar
¼ cup brown sugar
2 tablespoons water
⅓ cup Karo syrup
2 tablespoons butter or margarine
¼ cup unsweetened chocolate (also called chocolate
   liquor; melt before adding)
½ cup evaporated milk
¼ cup marshmallow topping
⅓ cup chopped walnuts or toasted almonds
½ teaspoon salt
¼ teaspoon vanilla flavor
*Large baking sheet for creaming the batch, lightly
   moistened with water just before the batch is poured
   on
*Baking pan, about 8×12×2 inches, lined with lightly
   greased wax paper

Follow the procedure for *Vanilla Fudge*. The unsweetened
chocolate is added to the boiling batch along with the butter
or margarine, before the milk is added.

PENUCHE FUDGE AND PENUCHE CHOCOLATE BARS

1¼ cups white sugar
¼ cup brown sugar
2 tablespoons water
⅓ cup Karo syrup
2 tablespoons butter or margarine
¾ cup evaporated milk

½ cup *Basic Buttercreme* or *Basic Fondant* (sugar crème)
¼ cup marshmallow topping
⅓ cup shredded coconut
⅓ cup chopped Brazil nuts
¼ teaspoon salt
¼ teaspoon butterscotch flavor
¼ teaspoon rum flavor
*Baking pan, about 8×12×2 inches, lined with lightly greased wax paper

Put the sugar, water, and Karo syrup into a pot and on the stove at medium heat and stir. When the batch boils up for the first time, wash the sugar crystals down from the sides of the pot and the stirring paddle, and add the butter or margarine. When the batch boils up again, start adding the evaporated milk, a little at a time. Keep the batch boiling and stir vigorously. It should take 4–5 minutes for all the milk to be added. When all the milk is in, put the thermometer in the pot. Keep stirring the batch constantly, but carefully, with the thermometer. Cook to 242° F. Then take the pot from the fire and cool the batch down to 190° F. by setting the pot into a pan of cold water for a few minutes. Stir occasionally with a wooden paddle to cool the batch evenly. When the batch has cooled to 190° F., stir in the buttercrème or fondant and the remaining ingredients.

Spread the batch about ¾ inch thick in the pan lined with wax paper. Roughen the surface of the penuche by drawing the tip of a spatula or a palette knife over the surface in a criss-cross motion. Let the penuche cool and set completely. Then take it out of the pan, cut it into squares, and wrap them in wax paper or foil; or, cut the penuche into bars about 1 inch wide and about 3½ inches long, and dip them in chocolate. Wrap each bar in foil.

CHAPTER 9

Quickie Candies

(Made without cooking, using simple ingredients)

BASIC BATCH

 1 tablespoon Karo syrup
 ⅔ cup sweetened condensed milk
 4½–5 cups confectioners' powdered sugar, sifted
 *Medium-sized bowl
 *2 baking sheets, 1 plain and 1 covered with wax paper

Pour the Karo syrup and milk into a mixing bowl, stir with a wooden paddle, and add the powdered sugar little by little. If the batch should get too stiff for stirring before all the sugar is in, remove the batch from the bowl, put it on a baking sheet, and knead in the balance of the sugar. The batch should now be like firm dough. If the batch of some recipe is too soft for shaping centers after the additional ingredients are kneaded in, knead in a little more sifted powdered sugar, to firm the batch up a little.

 The weight of the finished basic batch will be about 1 pound, 11 ounces, or 27 ounces. The recipes given below are for one-third of the basic batch, or 9 ounces each, so three different kinds of quickie candies can be made with one basic batch. Of course, if you wish to make a larger batch of any kind, using two-thirds or the whole basic batch for one recipe, you may do so. Just multiply the additional ingredients by two or three. The finished candies can be eaten at once, but it is better to let them dry and stiffen up for a few hours or overnight. When the candies have dried, store them in a cellophane bag to keep them fresh and tender. However, they will taste best if they are not older than two weeks.

RUM-WALNUT CANDIES

⅓ (about 9 ounces) of the *Quickie Candies Basic Batch*
1 teaspoon cocoa powder
1 teaspoon rum flavor
Quartered walnut meats

Knead all ingredients except walnuts together, roll into a rope about 1 inch thick, and slice into even, candy-sized pieces. Roll these round first, then elongate slightly, and put them on the baking sheet covered with wax paper. Moisten the top of each piece slightly, and decorate each piece with quartered walnut on top.

COFFEE DOUGHNUTS

⅓ of the *Quickie Candies Basic Batch*
5 teaspoons instant coffee

Knead the ingredients together, roll into a rope about 1 inch thick, and slice into even, candy-sized pieces. Roll these round, then flatten them slightly, and punch a hole in the center of each with a round, pointed piece of wood. Set them on the baking sheet.

CHERRY CRÈMES

> ⅓ of the *Quickie Candies Basic Batch*
> 1 teaspoon cherry flavor
> ¼ teaspoon citric acid or 1 teaspoon lemon juice
> A few drops pink food color
> Halved candied cherries

Knead all ingredients except cherries together, roll into a rope about 1 inch thick, and slice into even, candy-sized pieces. Roll these round, then press slightly flat, and place on the baking sheet. Decorate each with one-half of a candied cherry.

OPERA CRÈMES

> ⅓ of the *Quickie Candies Basic Batch*
> 1 teaspoon vanilla flavor
> 2 tablespoons cocoa powder
> 3 tablespoons powdered sugar, sifted
> *Small plate

Knead the vanilla flavor into the basic batch, roll it into a rope about 1 inch thick, and cut into even, candy-sized pieces. Roll these into balls. Mix the cocoa powder with the sifted powdered sugar on a small plate and roll the opera crèmes in the mixture as soon as you have rolled them round. Then take them out of the plate and roll them lightly in your

Plate 3 Bonbon-coated pieces

hands again. Place them on the baking sheet covered with wax paper.

COCONUT BALLS

⅓ of the *Quickie Candies Basic Batch*
¼ cup shredded white coconut
1 teaspoon coconut flavor
1 teaspoon vanilla flavor
½ cup shredded white coconut, additional
*Small plate

Knead all the ingredients, except for the additional half cup of shredded coconut, together, roll into a rope, and slice into even, candy-sized pieces. Roll these round, then moisten them slightly by rolling them in moistened hands. Put the additional coconut in the plate and roll the moistened coconut balls in it immediately. Completely cover the pieces with coconut and set them on the baking sheet.

PEANUT BUTTER SQUARES

⅓ of the *Quickie Candies Basic Batch*
⅓ cup peanut butter
¼ teaspoon salt

Knead the ingredients together, then sprinkle a little powdered sugar on the baking sheet. Press the batch into a flat square, and roll it down about ½ inch thick with a rolling pin. Press parallel grooves, about ¼ inch apart, into the surface with the back of a long knife or a spatula. Cut the batch into 1 inch squares, and place them on the baking sheet covered with wax paper.

NUTTY GOODY

⅓ of the *Quickie Candies Basic Batch*
⅔ cup unsalted, chopped nut meats
½ teaspoon vanilla flavor
¼ teaspoon rum flavor

Knead the ingredients together, then sprinkle a little powdered sugar on the baking sheet. Press the batch into a flat square and roll it down ½ inch thick with a rolling pin. Cut it into 1-inch squares and place them on the baking sheet covered with wax paper.

MINT PATTIES

⅓ of the *Quickie Candies Basic Batch*
¼ teaspoon peppermint oil
A few drops green food color

Knead the ingredients together, roll into a rope about 1 inch thick, and cut it into even ½-inch slices. Roll these round, then gently press them into patties about ¼ inch thick, on the wax paper-covered baking sheet.

CHOCOLATE WHITE-DOTS

⅓ of the *Quickie Candies Basic Batch*
1½ tablespoons cocoa powder
½ teaspoon vanilla flavor
¼ teaspoon rum flavor

Cut off a small piece, about 1 ounce, of the basic batch and set aside for the white dots. Knead the remaining ingredients together, roll into a rope about 1 inch thick, and cut into even, candy-sized pieces. Roll these round, set them on the baking sheet covered with wax paper, and press down lightly in the center of the piece with your index finger, making a round impression in the top of the piece. Roll the white piece into a small rope, about ½ inch thick, and cut it into even ½-inch slices. Roll each small piece round, and press it into the impression in the top of a chocolate piece, as decor. If the white pieces should not stick well enough, moisten the tops of the chocolate pieces slightly, with a moistened index finger, just before placing the white pieces on top.

NEAPOLITANS

⅓ of the *Quickie Candies Basic Batch*
¼ teaspoon cherry flavor
A few drops pink food color
¼ teaspoon vanilla flavor
½ tablespoon cocoa powder
A few drops rum flavor

The basic batch should be quite firm for this recipe; if necessary, knead in some more sifted powdered sugar. Divide the basic batch into 3 equal parts.

PART 1, PINK: Knead in the cherry flavor and color light pink with a few drops of pink food color.

PART 2, WHITE: Knead in the vanilla flavor.

PART 3, CHOCOLATE BROWN: Mix in the cocoa powder and the rum flavor.

Sprinkle powdered sugar on the baking sheet, and with a rolling pin, roll each part out, to a long, flat piece, ½ inch thick, 1 inch wide, and about 5–6 inches long. Moisten the top of the pink piece lightly with water; put the white piece on top. Moisten the top of the white piece lightly with water; put the chocolate piece on top. Lightly roll lengthwise over the sandwiched pieces with the rolling pin, set the candy on edge, so that the three layers are visible on top, and again roll it lengthwise with the rolling pin, so that the candy is 1 inch high and 1 inch wide. Cut it into 1-inch slices and set these on the baking sheet covered with wax paper, to dry them and firm them up.

CHAPTER 10

Marzipan

PURE ALMOND PASTE

Marzipan is one of the oldest confections to have come from Europe. It is made from blanched almonds, very finely ground, and refined, with the addition of small amounts of sugar and water. A small amount of corn syrup is added, and then it is toasted to a light beige, firm paste, called pure almond paste.

To this pure almond paste, sometimes known as "base paste," powdered sugar or fondant, corn syrup, colors, flavors, and other ingredients are added to give the confection its final texture and taste. Heavy machinery and equipment are needed to produce the basic pure almond paste, and therefore, we must start our marzipan confections with purchased pure almond paste, or "base paste."

CHOCOLATE-COATED MARZIPAN PIECES

BASIC BATCH:

1 pound pure almond paste
1½ cups powdered sugar, sifted
3 tablespoons Karo syrup
*Baking sheet with borders

Mix and knead all ingredients together on the baking sheet; total weight of the basic batch will be 1½ pounds.

VANILLA:

Mix in ¾ teaspoon vanilla flavor, roll out flat on the baking sheet sprinkled with powdered sugar, using a rolling pin and rolling the batch to the thickness of about ½ inch. Cut it into pieces about ½×1 inch. Dip these in chocolate.

RUM:

Mix in ¾ teaspoon rum flavor or 1½ tablespoons rum or brandy, being sure to sprinkle your hands and the baking sheet with powdered sugar. Roll the batch into a rope about 1 inch thick. Cut it into ½-inch slices and form flat, oval pieces. Dip the pieces in chocolate and decorate each with a blanched almond half on top.

COFFEE-WALNUT:

Mix in 3 tablespoons of instant coffee, being sure to sprinkle your hands and the baking sheet with powdered sugar. Roll the batch into a rope about 1 inch thick. Cut it into ½-inch slices and form flat, oval pieces. Dip these in chocolate and decorate each with a half walnut on top.

If you wish to make all three kinds of centers with one 1½ pounds basic batch, divide the batch into 3 parts of ½ pound each and add only one-third of the amounts given for the additional ingredients.

MARZIPAN CONFECT

1 pound pure almond paste
1½ cups powdered sugar, sifted
3 tablespoons Karo syrup
1 teaspoon vanilla flavor
3–4 drops (not more) yellow food color
1 fresh egg white
*2 baking sheets without borders, 1 plain and 1 covered
  with wax paper

Mix and knead all of the ingredients except the egg white together on the plain baking sheet. Scrape the baking sheet clean, and then lightly sprinkle the baking sheet and your hands with powdered sugar. Cut the batch into 6 approximately equal parts and roll each part out into a rope, each to an even thickness of about 1¼ inches. Cut each rope into ½ inch thick slices, and make sure that all the sliced pieces have as nearly the same size as possible, so that they will toast evenly later on.

To form the pieces into the six different shapes, proceed as follows:

LITTLE LOAF: Roll round first, then into a loaf shape. Place it on the baking sheet covered with wax paper and flatten it slightly with the ball of your hand. To decorate, put a little groove near each end with a knife, and a little round dent in the center, using a toothpick. Place the pieces close together, so that they touch each other.

CROSS BUNS: Roll round first, then place on the wax paper next to the row of loaves. Put a deep cross groove in the top of the piece with a knife or the center part of a toothpick. Place the cross buns close together, also.

DOUGHNUT: Roll round first, then place the piece on the baking sheet and flatten slightly. Pick it up again and pierce the center with a round, pointed piece of wood, about the size of a sharpened pencil. Place the pieces on the baking sheet, close together and next to the cross buns.

SPIRAL: Roll round first, then roll out to a little rope about 3½ inches long on the baking sheet. Flatten the rope to a thickness of about ¼ inch, and the ends to about ⅛ inch. Roll this flattened rope together into a spiral and place it on the baking sheet.

"S" SHAPE: Start rolling out like the spiral, but roll each end of the flattened rope in a different direction, forming an "S". Place it on the baking sheet.

CURL: Start rolling out like the spiral, but roll each end of the flattened rope in toward the center, forming a double curl. Place it on the baking sheet.

Set the shaped marzipan confects aside overnight, at room temperature, to dry the tops of the pieces.

TOASTING AND GLAZING: Place the pieces made the day before, in rows and touching each other, in the center of the baking sheet covered with wax paper, if you have not done this already. All the pieces should be of the same height, so that they will toast (brown) evenly. If the pieces are of different heights, use two baking sheets covered with wax paper, and put the lower pieces on one and the higher pieces on the other; brown them separately.

Cut off the wax paper protruding from under the marzipan pieces, to keep from burning it. Set the broiler control in your oven at 350° F., and wait 5 minutes for it to heat up. Place the baking sheet in the broiler, about 4 inches below the gas flame of a gas stove, or 4 inches below the heating element of an electric stove, for 4½–6 minutes. Check a few times, to make sure that all the pieces get an even browning. If the pieces on one side or end of the baking sheet seem to be getting browner than those on the other, turn the sheet around after a few minutes. When the pieces are golden brown, not darker, remove them from the broiler and brush the tops with the egg white to glaze them. Let cool. Store the finished pieces in a closed container in a cool place, or wrap them in foil, to keep them fresh and tender.

MARZIPAN POTATOES

1 pound pure almond paste
1½ cups powdered sugar, sifted
3 tablespoons Karo syrup
1 teaspoon vanilla flavor
¼ teaspoon rum flavor
3–4 drops (not more) yellow food color

FOR THE "PEEL":

1 tablespoon cocoa powder
4 tablespoons sifted powdered sugar, additional
*Baking sheet

Mix and knead all of the ingredients, except the cocoa and additional powdered sugar, together on the baking sheet. Scrape the baking sheet clean again, and lightly sprinkle your hands and the baking sheet with powdered sugar. Roll the batch into a rope about 1¼ inches thick and cut the rope into slices ½ inch thick.

Mix the cocoa powder and the 4 tablespoons of powdered sugar in a small dish. Place a small, clean dish towel on the table. Roll about 12 marzipan slices round and place them in the center of the dish towel. Sprinkle about 1 teaspoonful of the cocoa mixture over the pieces. Fold the towel together lengthwise, over the pieces, and gather the two ends of the towel in your hands. Lift the towel from the table and shake it from side to side, so that the marzipan pieces in the towel roll and are completely covered with the cocoa mixture. Place the towel back on the table, unfold, and again roll each piece in your hands for a moment. Make 2 or 3 cuts, close together, in the "peel" of each piece with a small knife, to simulate the cracked peel of a baked potato. Repeat this procedure, until all of the potatoes are done. For a variation, you can leave some of the pieces without cracks in the peel, or put a few "eyes" in the potato, with a pointed piece of wood. Keep the potatoes fresh and tender in a covered tin, or wrap them in foil.

SUMMARY

The recipes given in this chapter on marzipan are the most popular and convenient ones for making at home. There are, indeed, many more ways of making marzipan confections, but one needs quite a number of special tools and molds, and a great deal of craftsmanship, to make them. The variety of marzipan confections is so great, from simple pieces up to veritable masterpieces of art, that I could fill another book with the recipes for them. But again, it would be of interest mainly to professionals.

11

Fruit and Mint Jellies, Made with Agar-agar

BASIC AGAR JELLY BATCH

⅓ cup (¼ ounce) flake agar-agar
1 cup warm water
1 cup white sugar
¾ cup Karo syrup
Color and flavor as indicated below
*Use a larger pot than usual, because agar jelly boils up high
*Baking sheet with borders, lined with brown wrapping paper

Soak the agar-agar flakes in the warm water for 1 hour or longer, or even overnight, in a measuring cup or a glass jar. Sometimes agar-agar comes in long strips, rather than flakes. If you use agar-agar strips, make flakes out of them by cutting the strips into ¼-inch or shorter pieces with a pair of scissors, and weigh, rather than measure them.

Pour the soaked agar into a pot on low heat on the stove and stir gently until it boils. By now, the agar should have dissolved completely, but check; if there should still be some undissolved pieces, heat and stir 1 or 2 minutes longer. Then turn off the heat, add the sugar and Karo syrup, stir together, and put the pot back on the stove, at medium heat. When the batch boils up again, take out the stirring paddle, put in the thermometer, and cook to 222° F. Take the pot from the stove and set it in the sink, which should have about 2 inches of cold water in it. Stir the batch gently with the thermometer from time to time, until the jelly has cooled to 160° F. Add the colors and flavors, as indicated below, stir them in, and pour the batch onto the baking sheet lined with brown paper, making the batch about ¼–⅜ inch thick. If your baking sheet is too big, crease the paper to form a low border across the baking sheet, preventing the jelly from setting too low by flowing over the whole surface of the baking sheet with borders. Let the jelly set overnight in a cool room or in the refrigerator. Next day, take the jelly out of the tray and cut it, while it is still on the paper, into square or rectangular candy-sized pieces. Use a knife for this, and dip it repeatedly in hot water.

NEAPOLITAN JELLIES

Make 1 batch of one of the following agar jelly recipes and pour it out over the whole surface of the paper-lined baking sheet with borders, but not less than ⅛ inch thick. Let it set ½ hour or longer in the refrigerator; make another batch of agar jelly of a different flavor, but add ⅓ cup of marshmallow topping to it at the same time the color and flavor are added; and pour the second batch over the first. Let this set in the refrigerator for at least ½ hour, then make a third batch of agar jelly, but without marshmallow topping, and pour it over the top of the second layer. Let set overnight, then take the jelly out of the tray and cut it, while still on the paper, into candy-sized pieces, or else cut it into bar sizes, about 1 inch wide and 3½ inches. long.

SUGAR-SANDED JELLIES

Wet the surface of the cut batch of jelly very lightly, but evenly, with cold water. Cover with granulated white sugar. Turn the batch upside down, wet the paper with cold water, let soak a minute or two, then peel the paper off. Separate and roll the pieces in granulated sugar, sift off the surplus sugar, and let the pieces dry overnight at room temperature. Next day, put the finished jellies into a cellophane bag or covered jar, to keep them fresh and tender.

CHOCOLATE-COATED JELLIES

Proceed in the same manner as described for sugar-sanded jellies, but use flour instead of granulated sugar. The pieces do not have to be dried after the surplus flour is sifted off; you can dip them in chocolate right away.

MINT JELLIES

To the *Basic Agar Jelly Batch*, after being cooled to 160° F., add:

> ¼ teaspoon peppermint oil
> Enough green food color or paste to give a light green color
> ⅓ cup marshmallow topping (optional; for use in *Neapolitan Jellies*)
> Chopped walnuts or pecans (optional)

LEMON JELLIES

To the *Basic Agar Jelly Batch,* after being cooled to 160° F., add:

> ½ teaspoon lemon juice
> ¼ teaspoon lemon flavor
> Enough yellow food color or paste to give a light yellow color
> ⅓ cup marshmallow topping (optional; for use in *Neapolitan Jellies*)
> Rind of ½ lemon, finely chopped (optional)

STRAWBERRY JELLIES

To the *Basic Agar Jelly Batch,* after being cooled to 160° F., add:

> ½ teaspoon lemon juice
> ½ teaspoon strawberry flavor
> Enough red food color or paste to give a light red color
> ⅓ cup marshmallow topping (optional; for use in *Neapolitan Jellies*)
> Chopped walnuts or pecans (optional)

GRAPE JELLIES

To the *Basic Agar Jelly Batch,* after being cooled to 160° F., add:

> ½ teaspoon lemon juice
> ¼ teaspoon grape flavor
> Enough purple food color or paste to give a light purple color
> ⅓ cup marshmallow topping (optional; for use in *Neapolitan Jellies*)

ORANGE JELLIES

To the *Basic Agar Jelly Batch,* after being cooled to 160° F., add:

- ½ teaspoon lemon juice
- ¼ teaspoon orange flavor
- Enough orange food color or paste to give a light orange color
- ⅓ cup marshmallow topping (optional; for use in *Neapolitan Jellies*)
- Rind of ½ orange, finely chopped (optional)

RASPBERRY JELLIES

To the *Basic-Agar Jelly Batch,* after being cooled to 160° F., add:

- ½ teaspoon lemon juice
- ½ teaspoon raspberry flavor
- Enough red food color or paste to give a light red color
- ⅓ cup marshmallow topping (optional; for use in *Neapolitan Jellies*)
- Chopped walnuts or pecans (optional)

CHAPTER *12*

Fruit and Mint Jellies, Made with Gelatine and Applesauce

BASIC APPLESAUCE JELLY

> 3 packages Knox unflavored gelatine (¾ ounce or 2 tablespoons)
> ½ cup cold water
> 2 cups applesauce
> 2 cups sugar
> *Baking pan, about 8×8 inches, with low borders, lined with brown paper; or larger baking pan for sticks or candy bars

Soak gelatine in the cold water, set aside.

Put the applesauce and sugar into a pot on the stove at medium high heat and stir. After it has boiled up well, keep boiling and stirring 10–12 minutes longer. Take from stove. Stir again 5–6 minutes for cooling the batch to about 170–180° F. Then, stir the soaked gelatine in, dissolving it completely in the batch. Add the color, flavor, or other ingredients, as indicated in the following recipes, and pour the batch onto the baking pan lined with brown paper. Spread the batch about ½ inch thick for regular candy pieces; or only ¼–⅜ inch thick for sticks or candy bars. If your baking sheet or pan should be too big, crease the brown paper to form a low border across the baking sheet, preventing the jelly from setting too low by flowing over the whole surface of the baking sheet or pan. Let the jelly set overnight in a cool room or in the refrigerator. Next day, take the jelly out of the tray, and while it is still on the paper, cut it into square or rectangular candy-sized pieces or into ¼×2½-inch pieces for sticks, or into 1×3-inch-long pieces for bars.

SUGAR-SANDED JELLIES

Proceed in the same manner as described for *Sugar-Sanded* (Agar) *Jellies*.

CHOCOLATE-COATED JELLIES

Proceed in the same manner as described for *Chocolate-Coated* (Agar) *Jellies*.

APPLE-NUT JELLIES

To the batch of *Basic Applesauce Jelly*, add:

   1½ teaspoons lemon juice or ½ teaspoon citric acid
   ⅔ cup chopped walnuts

Color light green, with green food color or paste.

CINNAMON-APPLE JELLIES

To the batch of *Basic Applesauce Jelly*, add:

¾ teaspoon cinnamon or ¼ teaspoon cinnamon flavor
⅔ cup chopped walnuts (optional)

Color light red, with red food color or paste.

LEMON JELLIES

To the batch of *Basic Applesauce Jelly*, add:

1½ teaspoons lemon juice or ½ teaspoon citric acid
½ teaspoon lemon flavor

Color light yellow, with yellow food color or paste.

MINT JELLIES

To the batch of *Basic Applesauce Jelly*, add:

¼ teaspoon peppermint oil

Color light green, with green food color or paste.

ORANGE JELLIES

To the batch of *Basic Applesauce Jelly*, add:

1½ teaspoons lemon juice or ½ teaspoon citric acid
½ teaspoon orange oil

Color light orange, with orange food color or paste.

RASPBERRY JELLIES

To the batch of *Basic Applesauce Jelly*, add:

1 teaspoon lemon juice or ¼ teaspoon citric acid
1 teaspoon raspberry flavor

Color pink, with pink food color or paste.

SANDWICH JELLY, GREEN AND WHITE

To the batch of *Basic Applesauce Jelly*, add:

¼ teaspoon peppermint oil

Divide batch into 2 equal parts, by pouring half of the batch into another pot.

PART I

Color light green, with green food color or paste; pour into the baking pan lined with brown paper. Spread jelly about ¼ inch thick. Put into refrigerator for ½ hour to preset.

PART II

Reheat lightly, by putting it back on the stove at low heat for a minute or two. Stir.

Add ⅓ cup of marshmallow topping, stir, and blend well together. Pour carefully over preset Part I and spread evenly. Put back into refrigerator overnight to set up firm.

SANDWICH JELLY, RED AND WHITE

To the batch of *Basic Applesauce Jelly*, add:

   1 teaspoon lemon juice or ¼ teaspoon citric acid
   1 teaspoon strawberry or raspberry flavor

Divide batch into 2 equal parts, by pouring half of the batch into another pot.

PART I

Color red, with red food color or paste; pour into the baking pan lined with brown paper. Spread jelly about ¼ inch thick. Put into refrigerator for ½ hour to preset.

PART II

Reheat lightly by putting it back on the stove at low heat for a minute or two. Stir.

Add ⅓ cup of marshmallow topping, stir, and blend well together. Pour carefully over preset Part I and spread evenly. Put back into refrigerator overnight to set up firm.

STRAWBERRY JELLIES

To the batch of *Basic Applesauce Jelly*, add:

 1 teaspoon lemon juice or ¼ teaspoon citric acid
 1 teaspoon strawberry flavor

Color red, with red food color or paste.

CHAPTER 13

Specialties

TENDER HONEY NOUGAT

PART I

>   3 tablespoons dried egg whites dissolved in ¼ cup cold water
>   *or* 3 fresh egg whites (No additional water is used. Separate the eggs very carefully, so that there is no trace of yolk left, or else they will not beat)
>   ½ cup white sugar
>   ½ cup Karo syrup
>   ½ cup honey

PART II

>   2 cups white sugar
>   ⅓ cup water
>   ¾ cup Karo syrup
>   2 tablespoons butter or margarine
>   1 cup chopped walnuts
>   *or* ½ cup chopped walnuts and ½ cup candied fruit
>   ¾ cup powdered sugar, sifted
>   ½ teaspoon salt
>   A few drops vanilla flavor

A few drops butterscotch flavor
*Extra large beating bowl
*Baking sheet with borders, about 10×14 inches, greased and
  well sprinkled with flour

PROCEDURE—PART I:

Soak and dissolve the egg whites in the water by stirring them
well with a fork from time to time, until all the egg white
is dissolved. This will take about 20 minutes. If you wish, you
may prepare the egg whites ahead of time and store them in
the refrigerator until they are needed. If fresh egg whites are
used, separate the eggs very carefully. Set aside, but not in the
refrigerator.

Put the sugar and Karo syrup into a pot on medium heat
and stir. When it boils up for the first time, wash the sugar
crystals down from the sides of the pot and the stirring
paddle. Put the thermometer into the pot and cook to
248° F. without further stirring. Then take from the heat
and add the cold honey.

Put the dissolved dry egg whites or the fresh egg whites
into a large beating bowl and beat stiff. Keep the beater going
and add the syrup, with the honey mixed in, very slowly in a
fine string, to the beating egg whites. Keep beating until it
is thoroughly mixed and *really* stiff.

PROCEDURE—PART II:

While Part I is beating, put the sugar, water, and Karo syrup
for Part II into a pot on medium heat and stir. Wash the
sugar crystals down from the sides of the pot and the stirring paddle when the batch boils up for the first time. Put the
thermometer in the pot and cook to 272° F. without further
stirring. Then take the batch from the fire and add it very
slowly, in a fine stream, to the beating Part I. When all of

Pouring tender honey nougat

Part II is in, beat 10 minutes longer on medium speed. Then take the beater out and stir in the butter or margarine, chopped nuts, and/or fruit, powdered sugar, salt, and flavor.

Pour the batch onto the greased and floured baking sheet and spread it out ½–¾ inch thick. Sprinkle some flour on top. You may go over the batch lightly with a rolling pin to

Spreading tender honey nougat

make the surface smooth and even. Cover the batch and baking sheet with wax paper and let it cool overnight in a cool room but not in the refrigerator. Next day, take the batch out of the sheet, brush off the excess flour, and cut it into squares or rectangular pieces, using a sawing motion of the knife. Wrap the finished pieces in cellophane or wax paper, or dip them in chocolate.

Tender honey nougat ready for cooling

CHOCOLATE NOUGAT

PART I

> 3 tablespoons dried egg whites dissolved in ¼ cup cold water *or* 3 fresh egg whites, carefully separated (no additional water)
> ½ cup white sugar
> ½ cup Karo syrup
> ½ cup honey

PART II

    2 cups white sugar
    ⅓ cup water
    ¾ cup Karo syrup
    2 tablespoons butter or margarine
    1 cup chopped walnuts
    ¾ cup sifted powdered sugar, mixed with ⅓ cup cocoa
       powder
    ½ teaspoon salt
    A few drops vanilla flavor
    A few drops butterscotch flavor
    *Baking sheet with borders, about 10×14 inches, greased and
       well sprinkled with flour

Follow the procedure for *Tender Honey Nougat*, and add the powdered sugar-cocoa mixture at the same time the butter or margarine, nuts, salt, and flavor are added.

ALMOND TOFFEE

    1 cup toasted, chopped almonds
    1½ cups white sugar
    ¼ cup water
    ⅓ cup Karo syrup
    8 ounces margarine*
    ½ teaspoon salt
    ¼ teaspoon baking soda
    1½ cups toasted, chopped almonds, additional
    *Greased baking sheet

Warm the first cup of toasted almonds in the oven at 175° F. and keep them there until they are needed. Put the sugar, water, and Karo syrup into a pot and on the stove at medium heat and stir. When it boils up for the first time, wash the sugar crystals down from the sides of the pot and the stirring paddle. Keep boiling and stir in the margarine.* When the margarine is completely melted, take out the stirring paddle. Put in the thermometer and cook to 290° F., stirring carefully with the thermometer. Then take the pot from the fire and stir in the salt, baking soda, and the one cup of warmed almonds with a dry stirring paddle.

Pour the batch onto the greased baking sheet, spreading it evenly and about ¼ inch thick. Move the sheet to a cooler spot on the table every few minutes to cool it evenly. Soon,

Scoring almond toffee

when the batch feels plastic, like caramel, run a palette knife or spatula under the batch to release it from the tray, turn the batch over, and score it with the palette knife, making parallel lines about ½ inch apart. Then turn the baking sheet 90° and score the batch in parallel lines 1–1¼ inches apart. Cool the scored batch near an open window or in a cool room, but not in the refrigerator, or it will get

---

* If you wish to use butter instead of margarine, be sure to add ¼ teaspoon of lecithin, necessary to bind the fat with the other ingredients. Margarine already contains lecithin.

Dipping setup for almond toffee

sticky. Soon the pieces will be firm and will come off the sheet easily. Break the pieces apart at the score lines.

Spread the additional 1½ cups of cold almond pieces on a baking sheet with borders or in a wide, flat bowl. Dip the toffee centers in chocolate and roll them in the almonds right away, or else sprinkle the almonds on top. When the chocolate on the toffee centers has set for a few minutes, they can be taken out and set on a baking sheet covered with wax paper, for cooling and to make room for more centers on the almonds. When the pieces are completely cool, you may either wrap them individually in foil or leave them unwrapped. Store them in a cellophane bag or closed jar or tin, in a cool place.

Dipping almond toffee

Covering with chopped, toasted almonds

Finished almond toffee
Some plain chocolate coated, some covered with chopped,
toasted almonds, and some foiled pieces

DIVINITY

3 tablespoons dried egg white dissolved in ¼ cup cold water
  or 3 fresh egg whites (no additional water)
2 cups white sugar
½ cup water
3 tablespoons Karo syrup
1 cup chopped walnuts
½ teaspoon butterscotch flavor
*Baking sheet covered with wax paper

Soak and dissolve the dried egg whites in the ¼ cup of cold water, stirring well. This will take about 20 minutes. If possible, it is better to dissolve the egg whites 1 or 2 hours ahead of time, or the day before. Keep the dissolved egg whites in the refrigerator if you dissolve them the day before. Beat them stiff and set them aside. If fresh egg whites are used, separate them very carefully and make sure that there is no trace of yolk in them, or they will not beat. No additional water is used. Beat them stiff and set them aside.

Put the sugar, water, and Karo syrup into a pot and on the stove at medium heat and stir. Wash the sugar crystals down from the sides of the pot and the stirring paddle when it boils up for the first time. Cook to 236° F. Then take ⅓ cup of this syrup out of the pot and add it slowly to the egg whites, beating continuously at medium speed. Cook the remaining syrup to 264° F. Add this to the egg whites and 236° F. syrup, still beating continuously at medium speed. Keep beating 12–15 minutes longer, until the batch looks dull. Remove the beater, and add the nuts and flavor. Spoon the batch out, in small pieces, onto a baking sheet covered

Spooning out divinity

with wax paper. When the pieces are set, which should be in a few hours, store them in a closed jar or cellophane bag. This will keep them fresh and tender for weeks.

For best results, the batch should still be fairly warm when finished, and the beating speed should never exceed medium.

BUTTERED CARAMEL POPCORN

½ cup whole toasted almonds
½ cup large pecan pieces
1 gallon popped corn (with unpopped grains removed)
1 cup white sugar
½ cup brown sugar
¼ cup water
1¼ cups Karo syrup
¼ cup sweetened, condensed milk
6 tablespoons butter or margarine
½ teaspoon salt
*Large pot or metal bowl
*Enough aluminum foil to cover 4–6 square feet of table

Mix the toasted almonds, the pecan pieces, and the popcorn in a large pot or metal bowl. Place this in the oven at 250° F. Stir occasionally to heat evenly. Hold in the oven until the caramel is ready.

Put the sugar, water, Karo syrup, and condensed milk into a small pot and on the stove at low to medium heat and stir. When it boils up for the first time, wash the sugar crystals down from the sides of the pot and the stirring paddle. Then put the thermometer in and keep stirring. When the batch had reached 275° F., add the butter. Cook to 280° F., still stirring, and take the pot from the fire and add the salt.

Spreading the caramel popcorn

Take the popcorn out of the oven and add the caramel a little at a time, stirring the popcorn vigorously with a wooden paddle. Get all the caramel in quickly, though, or else the caramel will get too stiff. When all the caramel is in the popcorn, spread it out on the foil on the table. As soon as it is cool, pack it into a polyethylene bag, or keep it in a well-closed cookie jar or tin.

Plate 4 An assortment of cordial cherries, and how they will look when cordialized. Don't they look delicious?

Finished buttered caramel popcorn

FRENCH WHIPPED-CREAM TRUFFLES

2½ cups chocolate
½ pint whipping cream
¼ teaspoon salt
½ teaspoon rum flavor or a few drops vanilla flavor
About ¾ cup chocolate decorettes, for use when centers are
  dipped
*Baking sheet covered with wax paper

Melt the chocolate and cool it to 98–100° F. Keep it at this
temperature until needed. You may use dark or milk chocolate, depending on which you prefer. Whip the cream fairly
stiff, until it will hold a low peak. Then take the beater
from the bowl and add the chocolate, a little at a time, while
stirring vigorously with a stirring paddle. When all the chocolate is blended in, stir in the salt and flavor and put the beating bowl into the refrigerator.

When the batch in the bowl has set, beat it fluffy with a
stirring paddle. Beat it only long enough for the batch to

Filling a paper cone with truffle paste   *Closing*

become soft and smooth. Keep it cool. It should not get too soft and *not* runny. To form the centers for dipping, put part of the batch into a cone made from strong wrapping paper or locker wrap paper, or into a decorating bag with a round tip about ⅜–½ inch in diameter. Squeeze out even, round pieces, about the size of a quarter and about ¾ inch high side by side and in rows on the baking sheet covered with wax paper. Then put more of the batch into another cone or

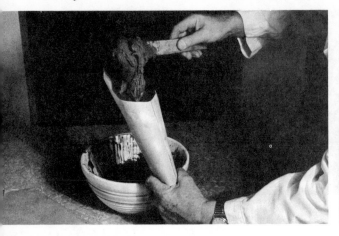

Forming truffle centers   *Truffle cen*

ber cone tightly   *Cutting the outlet tip of cone to correct size*

refill the decorating bag and continue until all the batch
has been squeezed into centers. Put the baking sheet with the
centers into the refrigerator for 1–3 hours, or in a cool place
overnight. When the centers are firm, dip them in chocolate
and sprinkle chocolate decorettes on top before the chocolate has set up. Keep the finished truffles in a cool place in a
closed jar, box, or tin.

dy for cooling   *Sprinkling decorettes on dipped truffle centers*

COCONUT MOUNDS

Two batches of *Fondant*, total weight about 2 pounds, 4 ounces

VANILLA COCONUT MOUNDS:

⅓ (about 12 ounces) of above *Fondant*
½ cup finely shredded white coconut
¼ teaspoon coconut flavor
¼ teaspoon vanilla flavor
¼ cup (1 heaping tablespoon) marshmallow topping
¼ teaspoon dry yeast dissolved in ½ teaspoon warm water

STRAWBERRY COCONUT MOUNDS:

⅓ (12 ounces) of above *Fondant*
½ cup finely shredded white coconut
½ teaspoon strawberry flavor
¼ teaspoon citric acid
A few drops pink food color
¼ cup marshmallow topping
¼ teaspoon dry yeast dissolved in ½ teaspoon warm water

CHOCOLATE COCONUT MOUNDS:

⅓ (12 ounces) of above *Fondant*
½ cup finely shredded white coconut
2 tablespoons cocoa powder (mix well with the coconut before adding)
¼ teaspoon rum flavor
¼ cup marshmallow topping
¼ teaspoon dry yeast dissolved in ½ teaspoon warm water
*Baking sheet covered with wax paper

Put the fondant, cut into small pieces, into a pot and on low heat. Remelt the fondant, stirring it until smooth and soft. Then replace the stirring paddle with the thermometer and keep stirring gently with the thermometer until the melted fondant is heated to 160° F. Take the pot from the fire, remove the thermometer, and stir in the coconut, flavor, color, marshmallow topping, and yeast with a wooden paddle. Let the batch cool in the pot until fairly stiff, and then, using 2 teaspoons, spoon mounds out onto the baking sheet covered with wax paper, as was done for *Divinity*. Do each flavor of coconut mounds separately. The three flavors will yield 25–30 pieces each, for a total of 75–90 pieces. When the pieces have set, store them in a covered cookie jar or cellophane bag.

SALT-WATER TAFFY

1½ cups white sugar
2 cups Karo syrup
4 tablespoons (½ stick) margarine
½ teaspoon salt
*Greased baking sheet
Colors and flavors as indicated below

Put the sugar and Karo syrup into a pot and place on the stove at medium heat and stir. When it boils up for the first time, wash the sugar crystals down from the sides of the pot and the stirring paddle. Stir in the margarine. Cook to 248° F. without further stirring. Then take the pot from the stove and stir in the salt. Pour the batch onto the greased baking sheet.

When the batch has cooled off for 3–4 minutes, put the

color and flavor on the batch and fold the edges of the batch into the center to form a square mass. Move the batch to a cooler spot on the sheet, turn it over, and fold in the edges again. Repeat 3 or 4 times. This cools the batch evenly and mixes in the color and flavor.

When the batch is cool enough to handle, but still soft and plastic, form a rope about 2 inches thick. Pull the rope until it is 2–3 feet long and fold in half. Then twist the rope and repeat. Pull the taffy in this manner for about 20 minutes. Finally, stretch it into a rope ¾ inch thick on a clean table and cut it into ¾-inch-long pieces with a pair of scissors. Wrap the pieces in wax paper.

For variety, one can also sandwich 2 or more finished, pulled ropes of different colors together, and stretch them into a single rope ¾ inch thick, for multicolored pieces.

The following amounts of colors and flavors are suggested per batch of salt-water taffy, but you may experiment with different color-flavor combinations if you wish. To use a single batch for more than one color of taffy, divide the batch and the amounts given by the appropriate number, and pull them separately. Paste food colors are recommended for use in taffy, since they will give stronger colors without adding the water that is present in liquid food colors. However, liquid food colors can be used.

White Taffy — 2 teaspoons vanilla flavor, no color

Yellow Taffy — 1 teaspoon lemon oil, a few drops yellow color or paste

Orange Taffy — 1 teaspoon orange oil, a few drops orange color or paste

Pink Taffy — 1 teaspoon raspberry or strawberry flavor, pink color or paste

Green Taffy — 1 teaspoon peppermint oil, green color or paste

Brown Taffy — 1 teaspoon rum flavor, 4 tablespoons cocoa powder

Finally, an interesting variation in texture can be produced in the taffy by adding ½ cup of finely shredded white coconut to the taffy along with the color and flavor and pulling as usual, though you must make sure that not too much of the coconut falls from the rope while it is being pulled.

PECAN ROLLS

1 batch *Milk Caramel*, cooked to the *firm ball* stage (firmer than for regular caramels)

1 cup *Fondant*
¼ cup marshmallow topping
4–6 cups chopped pecans
1 batch *Milk Caramel* cooked to the *soft ball* stage
*4 baking sheets with borders, 1 greased well and sprinkled well with flour, 1 lined with wax paper and sprinkled with powdered sugar, 1 plain, 1 lined with wax paper
*Bread pan

PART I:

Cook 1 batch of caramel to the *firm ball* stage, but leave the caramel in the pot and cool it to 175–180° F. Stir in the fondant and the marshmallow topping. Then pour the batch onto the well-greased and flour-sprinkled baking sheet. Spread it out about ¾ inch thick and about 5 inches wide. Cool the batch for several hours or overnight in the refrigerator, until it is firm enough to handle; take batch out of baking sheet, and place batch on a cutting board, sprinkled lightly with flour. Cut the cooled batch into strips about ¾ inch wide,

Making pecan rolls; cutting the centers

cutting parallel to the 5-inch width. Use a sawing motion of the knife to prevent sticking. Put the cut strips back into the refrigerator on a sugar-sprinkled baking sheet to stiffen up again before dipping.

PART II:

Spread the chopped pecans on the plain baking sheet, quite densely and at least ½ inch deep. Cook the second batch of caramel to the *soft ball* stage and pour it into the bread pan, or a similar container about 4 inches wide, 6–7 inches long, and with sides 2–3 inches high. Keep it hot on the stove at very low heat until you are just about to dip the centers.

Place the baking sheet with the nuts in the center of the table and place the baking sheet lined with wax paper to the right of it. Then take the center strips out of the refrigerator and place them to the left of the nut sheet. Take the bread pan from the stove and place it on the table directly in front

Dipping the centers in hot caramel and rolling them in pecans

of you, in front of the nut sheet. Then take one of the center strips off the sheet on your left and drop it in the bread pan, so that it is completely submerged. You may have to tilt the bread pan for this. Using 2 forks, lift the center strip out of the caramel, let the surplus caramel drip off, and place the strip on the nut sheet. Roll the dipped center in the pecans until it is completely covered. Finally, lift it out of the pecan sheet and place it on the baking sheet lined with wax paper. Do this with each of the centers. Move the finished

Finished pecan rolls and slices

rolls close together on the baking sheet so that they will keep their shapes, and cool them in the refrigerator for several hours or overnight. When they are firm, move them apart and shape each of them into a round roll in your hands. Cut the pecan rolls into slices ½–¾ inch thick, but slice only as much as will be eaten soon, so that the rest will stay fresh and tender. Keep the unsliced rolls wrapped in foil or wax paper in a cool, dry place.

CANDIED FRUIT PEEL

½ pound lemon peel, or ½ pound orange peel, or ½ pound grapefruit peel, or a combination of the three, totaling ½ pound

First day: 2 cups sugar
      1 cup water   Cook to 220° F.
Second day: ¼ cup sugar
      ¼ cup Karo syrup   Cook to 222° F.
Third day: ¼ cup sugar
      ¼ cup Karo syrup   Cook to 226° F.
Fourth day: ¼ cup sugar
      ⅓ cup Karo syrup   Cook to 230° F.

Total ingredients for syrup:

2¾ cups white sugar
1 cup water
¾ cup+2 tablespoons Karo syrup
*China or stainless steel bowl

FIRST DAY: Peel lemons, oranges, or grapefruit carefully, using a short, pointed knife to cut about ¼ inch deep all around the fruit; cut the peel into 4–6 sections and take it off with your fingers. Cut the sections into strips ⅜–½ inch wide and 2–3 inches long, or into oblong shapes about ½ inch wide and 1 inch long. Wash and rinse the peels in cold water.

Put the pieces into a pot, and add enough water to cover, when they are pushed down into the pot, and put the pot on the stove at medium heat. When the water begins to boil, reduce the heat and let simmer for 25 minutes. Take the peels from the stove, strain off the hot water, and hold the strainer with the peels under cold running water for a minute. Put the peels back into the pot and fill it with cold water, and set aside.

Put the 2 cups of sugar and 1 cup of water into a pot and on the stove at medium heat. Wash the adhering sugar crystals down from the sides of the pot and the stirring paddle when the batch boils up for the first time. Put the thermometer in the pot and cook to 220° F. Strain all the water from the peels and add them to the cooked syrup in the pot. Put the pot back on the stove at medium heat and boil it up once. Then pour the batch into the china or stainless steel bowl. Completely cover the surface of the batch with a piece of wax paper, directly on top of the peels and syrup, in order to keep in the heat as long as possible. Set the bowl aside at room temperature for 24 hours.

SECOND DAY: Remove the wax paper from the bowl and pour the whole batch into a small pot. Put it on the stove at medium heat and boil up once, stirring carefully. Strain the syrup from the peels. Put the syrup back into the pot; wash and dry the bowl and put the drained peels back into it.

Add ¼ cup of sugar and ¼ cup of Karo syrup to the syrup in the pot, stir, and cook to 222° F. Pour the hot syrup over the peels in the bowl, cover the surface of the batch with wax paper, and set aside at room temperature until the next day.

THIRD DAY: Repeat the procedure as described for the second day, adding ¼ cup of sugar and ¼ cup of Karo syrup to the syrup and cooking it to 226° F.

FOURTH DAY: Repeat the procedure as described for the second day, adding ¼ cup of sugar and ⅓ cup of Karo syrup to the syrup and cooking it to 230° F. But then, put the peels back into the pot, boil it up once, and pour the batch into a 1-quart Mason jar or similar glass container with a wide opening. Cover the surface of the batch in the jar with another piece of wax paper, but do not close the jar itself until the next day, when the batch has cooled, to prevent condensation of moisture in the jar. The peels are now preserved, and can be kept this way in a cool place until needed.

To prepare the peels for chocolate dipping, pour the peels and the syrup back into a pot and on the stove at low heat and stir carefully, until the syrup boils up again. Drain the peels and place them on a screen or a wire rack, with the help of two forks, while the pieces are still hot, to permit all the syrup to drop off. Set aside overnight, or until cool and dry enough for dipping in chocolate.

The remaining syrup has an excellent, natural citrus fruit flavor and can be used, slightly thinned down with hot water, on pancakes and waffles.

PRALINE

Praline is one of the most popular confections that has come from France; smooth and creamy, with the natural flavor of toasted filberts, one of its main ingredients. However, to make praline as smooth as it should be, very heavy machinery is needed, for refining the ingredients, and therefore, praline made at home will be coarser than the real product. Nevertheless, it will taste delicious.

1½ cups white sugar
1 cup raw filberts
1½ cups melted milk chocolate
1 teaspoon vanilla flavor
¼ teaspoon salt
*Greased baking sheet
*Baking sheet with borders, lined with wax paper

Put the sugar and raw filberts into a small frying pan (about 7–7½ inches across), without water, on medium heat and stir with a wooden paddle. Little by little, the sugar will melt, and will toast the filberts at the same time. This will take 10–12 minutes, depending on how fast the filberts toast. Keep stirring, and when the filberts are a light golden brown, take the pan from the heat and pour the batch onto the greased baking sheet. You can scrape the pan out with the wooden paddle you used for stirring the batch.

When the batch has cooled for a few minutes, move it to a cooler spot on the greased baking sheet, using a greased steel spatula. Let cool several minutes longer, then turn the batch over and again put it on a cooler spot on the baking sheet. Let cool until completely hard. This may take ½ hour or longer, depending on the temperature of the room. Do not put the batch into the refrigerator to cool, or it will get sticky.

When the batch is cold, break it into small pieces and run it through a very fine meat grinder 5 or 6 times. If your meat grinder has several grinding plates, use the one with the finest holes. The closer the ground batch is to a smooth paste, the better.

Put the ground paste into a mixing bowl, add the melted milk chocolate, which should be cooled to 90° F., and the salt and flavor. Stir well, then pour the batch out onto the baking sheet covered with wax paper, spreading it about 1 inch thick. Put this into the refrigerator to cool and set. This will take about 1 hour or longer, but check from time to time. When the batch is firm enough, like hard butter, take the baking sheet out of the refrigerator, turn the batch upside down, and take off the wax paper. Knead the batch together, being sure to sprinkle your hands and the baking sheet with powdered sugar to prevent sticking. Roll the batch out into a rope, about 1 inch thick, cut it into uniform pieces, and roll these into ball shapes, not larger than ¾ inch in diameter.

Set the shaped centers on a baking sheet covered with wax paper. Put them back into the refrigerator, or cover the centers with a sheet of wax paper and set them in a cool room overnight, to firm them up enough for dipping in chocolate. (Use a cherry dipping fork for this.) Should the batch get too soft while you are kneading or shaping it, put it back into the refrigerator awhile, to firm up again.

For square or oblong pieces, spread the finished batch only ½ inch thick on the baking sheet covered with wax paper. Put it into the refrigerator until the batch has set firm. Take it out of the refrigerator and cut it into pieces with a knife, which you should dip into hot water frequently, and wipe dry, to prevent sticking. Then cover the batch with wax paper and put it back into the refrigerator for about 1 hour, or in a cold room overnight, for the final setting. Break the pieces apart and dip them in chocolate.

CHAPTER **14**

Cordials

NOTE: The sale of cordial candies containing alcohol is prohibited in the United States, according to Federal law. This law, of course, does not apply to non-alcoholic cordials, the recipes for which follow the section on alcoholic cordials.

ALCOHOLIC FRUIT CORDIALS

1–2 pounds fruit, soaked in alcohol as described either in Part I (A) or (B)

Alcohol in which the fruit was soaked

2 batches *Fondant,* made one or several days before, well cooled, and then wrapped in foil or cellophane to hold until needed

Appropriate flavor (cherry flavor, for cherries; pineapple flavor, for pineapple; rum flavor, for peaches; or strawberry flavor, for strawberries)

2 pounds milk or bittersweet chocolate coating

*1-quart Mason jar, or other quart jar with an airtight cover

*2 baking sheets covered with wax paper

*For dipping the cordials in fondant and chocolate, use a cherry dipping fork, which has a round ring on the dipping end. The regular dipping fork, with open parallel prongs, is not suited for dipping cordials.

PART I (A): Soaking and preparing *canned* fruit for cordials, at least 2 weeks in advance:

> 1–2 pounds canned fruit, drained (canned pie cherries or canned sliced pineapple or canned peaches or frozen strawberries); do not mix the fruit, use only one kind.
> Brandy, rum, or other hard liquors

Drain all the syrup or juice from the canned fruit; the frozen strawberries, of course, must be completely thawed before being drained. Cut the pineapple into wedges, not more than ¾ inch wide at the outside edge; cut the peaches into small, bite-sized pieces. Remember, the finished candies will be almost twice the size of the fruit centers. Put the fruit into the Mason jar or any other glass container with an air-tight cover. Mix 2 parts of brandy with 1 part of rum and pour this over the fruit in the jar, about 1 inch higher than the top of the fruit. Close the jar tightly and set it aside at room temperature, not in the refrigerator. Let soak for at least 2 weeks, longer if possible. Shake gently every few days, to help the alcohol penetrate the fruit. Depending on your own taste, you may also use one or a combination of other hard liquors, like whiskey, vodka, or gin, for soaking the fruit.

PART I (B): Soaking and preparing *fresh* fruit for cordials, at least 3–4 weeks in advance:

The use of fresh fruit is preferable to canned or frozen fruit, because cordials made from fresh fruit will have a slightly higher alcoholic content when finished than those made with fruit originally prepared with sugar syrup, when it was canned. Use:

1–2 pounds fresh fruit (sour pie cherries or fresh pineapple or fresh peaches or fresh strawberries); do not mix the fruit, use only one kind.
Brandy, rum, or other hard liquors

Cherries: Wash, drain, remove the stems, but leave the pits in. The cherries should be pitted just before dipping.

Fresh pineapple: Peel, remove the core, cut into slices about ¼–⅜ inch thick, cut the slices into wedges about ¾ inch wide at the outside edge.

Fresh peaches, ripe, but not soft: Submerge in boiling water for a minute or two (scald), peel, cut in half, remove pit, cut the fruit into small, bite-sized pieces, not larger than a ¾-inch cube.

Fresh strawberries, ripe but firm: Select small-sized strawberries; if this is not possible, cut them into bite-sized pieces, not larger than a ¾-inch cube.

Remember that the finished cordials will be about twice the size of the fruit centers.

Put the fruit into a Mason jar or other glass container with an airtight cover. Mix 2 parts of brandy with 1 part of rum and pour this over the fruit in the jar, about 1 inch higher than the top of the fruit. Again, depending on your own taste, you may also use one or a combination of other hard liquors, like whiskey, vodka, or gin, for soaking the fruit. Close the jar tightly and set it aside at room temperature, not in the refrigerator. Let soak for at least 3–4 weeks, longer if possible. Shake gently every few days, to help the alcohol penetrate the fruit.

PART II: Dipping the fruit in fondant and putting on the chocolate bottoms:

Drain the fruit well, but save the "fruit liquor" (the alcohol in which the fruit was soaked). Place the drained fruit on a paper towel, to dry the surface. Pit the cherries.

Cut the fondant into small pieces. Put about one-third of the fondant into a small saucepan. Put it on the stove at low heat and add about 1 tablespoon of the fruit liquor. Stir until all of the fondant is melted. Then add some more pieces of fondant, melt them, add more pieces, melt them, etc., until about two-thirds of the fondant is in the saucepan and is melted. Take great care to make sure that the fondant in the saucepan never gets hotter than 160° F. If the fondant in the saucepan does get hotter than 160° F., take the saucepan from the heat for a while and continue melting the fondant off the stove. Then return it to the stove when the temperature goes below 160° F.

Add a few drops of the appropriate flavor to the melted fondant. The consistency of the fondant at 160° F. should now be like that of thick pea soup. If it is too thin, add some more cold fondant; if it is too thick, add a little more fruit liquor. Then take the saucepan from the stove.

Using the cherry dipping fork, dip one piece of fruit in the melted fondant and set it on the wax paper on the baking sheet. If the fondant sets up dry in about 1 minute, so that you can lift the piece off the wax paper easily, without the bottom sticking on the paper, your fondant is ready for dipping. If the dipped fruit looks shiny and sticks to the paper, add a little more fondant, reheat to 160° F., and try again. When the test-dipped piece sets up well, proceed with the dipping.

While preparing the fondant for dipping, also melt about 2 pounds of chocolate in a double boiler and start to precool some of it for tempering.

Dip only 20–30 of the cherries or fruit pieces in the fon-

Put cherry into fondant; cover and lift out; set on wax paper

dant at a time, and cool them near an open window or in the refrigerator (but only for 5–10 minutes). While the fondant-dipped pieces are cooling, temper about ½ pound of the chocolate. Many of the fondant-dipped pieces, especially at the beginning, while you are still learning, will have bottoms that are too large. Trim any fondant bottoms that are too large with a small knife before putting on the chocolate bottoms.

Now take one of the fondant-coated fruit pieces between two or three fingertips and dip it about ¼ inch deep in the tempered chocolate, forming a chocolate bottom. Lift the piece out of the chocolate and wipe the surplus chocolate off on the rim of the baking sheet containing the chocolate. This is to make sure that the chocolate bottom is no wider

Dip bottom only; wipe surplus chocolate off; set on wax paper

than the piece itself. Set the piece on a baking sheet covered
with wax paper.

Dip all the fondant-dipped pieces in this manner and set
the baking sheet near an open window or in the refrigerator
(but only for 5–10 minutes) to cool and set the chocolate
bottoms.

Stir and reheat the fondant in the saucepan. Add some
more cold fondant, a little fruit liquor, and a few drops of
flavor. As before, be careful not to heat the fondant over
160° F. Test it again by dipping a single piece of fruit, and if
it sets up firmly, proceed with dipping the rest of the fruit
pieces, 20–30 at a time. Cool these pieces and put chocolate
bottoms on them also.

PART III: Dipping cordial fruit in chocolate:

When the chocolate bottoms on all of the fruit pieces are
well cooled, so that they come off the wax paper easily, dip

Put into chocolate, bottom up; cover and lift out; form spiral decoration on top

the fruit centers in tempered chocolate. Submerge the center, bottom up, in the chocolate. Then follow the procedure of taking off the surplus chocolate, as outlined in the section on chocolate dipping, though the cherry dipping fork has a loop instead of prongs.

When the coated piece is set on the cooling sheet, gather some chocolate from the top of the piece into the loop of the cherry dipping fork and let this chocolate run over the top of piece in a circular motion, forming a small spiral—the typical cherry decor—on top of the piece. This, of course, takes some practice, but if you do not succeed the first time, try again. The decor is just for appearance, anyway, and has no bearing on the taste of the finished piece. Cool the finished, dipped pieces as outlined in the section on chocolate dipping.

Keep the chocolate-dipped cordials in a covered box or tin in a fairly cool place for a while, before starting to eat them.

The liquor will cordialize the fondant almost completely in one or two weeks.

PART IV: What to do with the flavored dipping fondant left over:

Stir and reheat the fondant to 160° F. Add any cold fondant left over, plus some food coloring. Stir until the fondant is completely melted and is uniformly colored, making sure that it never gets hotter than 160° F.

Drop small amounts of the fondant onto a baking sheet covered with wax paper, using a teaspoon and forming drops about the size of a half-dollar. When they are cold and firm, dip them in chocolate or leave them uncoated. NOTE: These drops will not cordialize, even if they are coated.

NON-ALCOHOLIC CORDIALS

1 can (about 1 pound) fruit in light syrup (pie cherries, peach halves or slices, pineapple slices, or pear halves)

Juice or syrup from the can

2 batches *Fondant*, made one or several days before, well cooled, and then wrapped in foil or cellophane to hold until needed

Dry or compressed yeast

Appropriate flavor (cherry flavor, peach flavor, pineapple flavor, or vanilla flavor, respectively)

2 pounds milk or bittersweet chocolate coating

*2 baking sheets covered with wax paper

*For dipping the cordials in fondant and chocolate, use a cherry dipping fork, which has a round ring on the dipping end. The regular dipping fork, with open parallel prongs, is not suited for dipping cordials.

PART 1: Dipping the fruit in fondant and putting on the chocolate bottoms:

Drain the fruit well, but save the juice. Cut the peach halves or slices, pineapple slices, or pear halves into small chunks about the size of a pie cherry. Place the drained and cut fruit on a paper towel, to dry the surface.

Cut the fondant into small pieces. Put about one-third of the fondant into a small saucepan. Put it on the stove at low heat and add about 1 tablespoon of fruit juice from the can. Stir until all of the fondant is melted. Then add some more pieces of fondant, melt them, and add more pieces and melt them, until about two-thirds of the fondant is in the saucepan and is melted. Take great care to make sure that the fondant in the saucepan never gets hotter than 160° F. Take the saucepan from the heat for a while and continue melting the fondant off the stove if it does. Then return it to the stove when the temperature goes below 160° F.

Dissolve ½ teaspoon of yeast in ¾ teaspoon of warm water. Stir the dissolved yeast and 1 teaspoon of the flavor into the dissolved fondant. The consistency of the fondant at 160° F. should now be like thick pea soup. If it is too thin, add some more cold fondant; if it is too thick, add some more of the fruit juice. Then take the saucepan from the stove.

Using the cherry dipping fork, dip one piece of fruit in the melted fondant and set it on the wax paper on the baking sheet. If the fondant sets up dry in about 1 minute, so that you can lift the piece off the wax paper easily, without the bottom sticking on the paper, your fondant is ready for dipping. If the dipped piece looks shiny and sticks to the paper, add a little more fondant, reheat to 160° F., and try again.

When the test-dipped piece sets up well, proceed with the dipping.

While preparing the fondant for dipping, also melt about 2 pounds of chocolate in a double boiler and start to precool some of it for tempering.

Dip only 20–30 of the fruit pieces in the fondant at a time, and cool them near an open window or in the refrigerator (but only for 5–10 minutes). While the fondant-dipped pieces are cooling, temper about ½ pound of the chocolate. Many of the fondant-dipped pieces, especially at the beginning, while you are still learning, will have bottoms that are too large. Trim any bottoms that are too large with a small knife before putting on the chocolate bottoms.

Now take one of the cooled fondant-coated pieces between two or three fingertips and dip it about ¼ inch deep in the tempered chocolate, forming a chocolate bottom. Lift the piece out of the chocolate and wipe the surplus chocolate off on the rim of the baking sheet containing the chocolate. This is to make sure that the chocolate bottom is not wider than the piece itself. Set the piece on another baking sheet covered with wax paper.

Dip all the pieces in this manner and set the baking sheet near an open window or in the refrigerator (but only for 5–10 minutes) to cool and set the chocolate bottoms.

Stir and reheat the fondant in the saucepan. Add some more cold fondant, ½–1 tablespoon of juice from the can, a few drops of flavor, and ¼ teaspoon of yeast dissolved in ½ teaspoon of warm water. As before, be careful not to heat the fondant over 160° F. Test it again by dipping a single piece, and if it sets up firm, proceed with dipping the rest of the fruit pieces. Cool these and put chocolate bottoms on them also.

PART II: Dipping the pieces in chocolate:

When the chocolate bottoms on all of the pieces are well cooled, so that they come off the wax paper easily, dip the centers into tempered chocolate. Submerge the center, bottom up, in the chocolate. Then follow the procedure for taking off the surplus chocolate, as outlined in the section on chocolate dipping, though the cherry dipping fork has a loop instead of prongs.

When the coated piece is on the cooling sheet, gather some chocolate from the top of the piece into the loop of your cherry dipping fork and let this chocolate run over the top of the piece in a circular motion, forming a small spiral— the typical cherry decor—on top of the piece. This, of course, takes some practice, but if you do not succeed the first time, try again. The decor is just for appearance and has no bearing on the taste of the finished piece. Cool the chocolate-dipped pieces as outlined in the section on chocolate dipping.

Keep the chocolate-dipped fruit in a covered box or tin in a fairly cool place for a while, before starting to eat them. The fondant will cordialize almost completely in one or two weeks.

PART III: What to do with the flavored dipping fondant left over:

Stir and reheat the fondant to 160° F. Add any cold fondant left over, plus some food coloring. Stir until the fondant is completely melted and is uniformly colored, making sure that it never gets hotter than 160° F.

Drop small amounts of the fondant onto a baking sheet covered with wax paper, using a teaspoon and forming drops about the size of a half-dollar. When they are cold and firm, dip them in chocolate or leave them uncoated. NOTE: These drops will not cordialize, even if they are coated.

Glossary

Agar-agar: Agar-agar is the dried substance of a gelatine like algae, growing in the Pacific and Indian oceans and in the Sea of Japan.

Almonds, blanching: Boil water in a medium-sized pot. Put raw almonds into the boiling water. Remove pot from fire. Let stand 3–4 minutes, drain the hot water from the almonds, and remove the husks by squeezing each almond between thumb and index finger. Put blanched almonds into a strainer, rinse with cold water, then spread on a baking sheet covered with a paper towel, for drying. Do not store blanched almonds before they are completely dry, or they will get moldy.

Almonds, roasting: With shortening, lightly grease a baking sheet with borders. Spread the raw almonds on the sheet, preheat the oven to 350° F. for 5 minutes, and put the sheet in the oven. Stir the almonds and shake the sheet slightly every few minutes. After 6–8 minutes, break one of the almonds open to check the inside; if light brown, remove the almonds from the oven. If still too light, leave them in the oven a few minutes longer, check again by breaking open another almond or two. When golden brown on the inside, remove almonds from oven and cool at room temperature before using or storing in a cellophane bag.

Baking soda: Pure sodium bicarbonate. Do not substitute baking powder.

Base paste: Pure almond paste, made from blanched almonds, small amounts of sugar, corn syrup, and water. Very finely ground and refined with heavy machinery, then toasted to a light beige, firm paste. Sold mainly in large cans containing 6–8 pounds.

Batch: The total mass of the candy being made, at the time specified.

Bonbon coating: In white and pastel colors; white coating can be colored with oil-soluble food colors or cocoa; DO NOT mix with chocolate. Does not need to be tempered; melt, cool down until part of the coating starts to set up on sides of pot, stir, and reheat again to 96–100° F. Start dipping.

Butter: Interchangeable with margarine, except in almond toffee, where a small amount of lecithin must be present to bind the fat to the rest of the batch. Not interchangeable with liquid cooking oils.

Buttercrème, creaming: See **Fondant, creaming.**

Caramel, cutting: Cut with a long knife, moving knife back and forth swiftly in a sawing motion, to prevent sticking.

Caramel, testing: Put a quart-sized saucepan in the sink and let a steady stream of cold water flow into it. Take ½ teaspoon of caramel out of pot, submerge in the cold water. After a moment, take it out of the spoon and try to roll into a ball, while still submerged. If it forms a ball of the desired consistency, the caramel is ready. If it does not form a ball or is too soft, cook and stir caramel for a few minutes longer, test again. If ball is too firm, add 2 tablespoons hot water to caramel, stir and boil up again, test again.

Chocolate, unsweetened: Bitter chocolate, also called chocolate liquor. Melt before adding. Substitution: 2½ tablespoons cocoa plus 1½ teaspoons additional margarine=1 ounce=1 square of unsweetened chocolate.

Chocolate dipping: Work in a cool room (65–68° F. is ideal). Put a center, bottom up, into the tempered chocolate, cover bottom of piece with chocolate gathered between prongs of dipping fork. Pick piece up with fork, lower it to surface of dipping chocolate, to remove excess, set right-side-up on baking sheet covered with wax paper. Decorate top of piece with prongs or points of fork prongs. For thin mints, put into dipping chocolate right-side-up, place on wax paper with fork beneath, slide fork out from under piece.

Chocolate melting: Use double boiler; the bottom and sides of upper pot should be submerged in the water. Heat water to 135–140° F., never higher. Cut chocolate into large pieces, melt by stirring from time to time. Be sure to wipe bottom and sides of upper pot dry before pouring out the chocolate.

Chocolate tempering: Work in a cool room (65–68° F.) Melt 2 pounds of chocolate coating in double boiler, pour about two-thirds out onto tray, cool it about 90° F. (It should feel neither warm nor cool on lower lip or wrist.) Add 1–2 heaping teaspoons grated chocolate (seeding), mix in, and cool until it feels cool on lower lip, temperature about 80–82° F.

Citric acid: Natural acid of citrus fruit juices, extracted and crystallized, or made chemically. Used mainly in hard candies, where moisture of lemon juice would spoil the product. Destroyed by heating over 180° F. Therefore, hard candy batch must be cooled below 180° F. and acid crystals folded in. Hard candy drops containing citric acid cannot be made without special machinery.

Coconut, shredded: Grate the coconut meat on rougher side of cheese grater. Spread on baking sheet with borders covered with wax paper. Put into oven at 300° F. for 10–12 minutes; stir from time to time. Remove from oven, cool off at room temperature before using or storing in cellophane bag or closed jar.

Coconut, toasting: Spread dry, shredded white coconut on baking sheet with borders, put into oven preheated to 350° F. Stir from time to time, also shake baking sheet to help brown coconut evenly. When coconut is light, golden brown, remove from oven and let cool at room temperature before using or storing in cellophane bag or closed jar.

Cordialize: To become liquid.

Dragées: For all dragée confections, such as Jordan almonds, Boston baked beans, jelly beans, jelly eggs, bridge mix, and M & M's, to name just a few, revolving dragée pans and polishing pans are needed. It is therefore impossible to make dragée confections at home.

Egg whites, dried: 3 tablespoons dried egg white plus ¼ cup cold water=3 fresh egg whites. Soak and completely dissolve dried egg whites in *cold* water; this takes about 20 minutes or longer, so it is best to dissolve them beforehand. Dissolved egg whites should be stored in refrigerator; dry powder need not be.

Egg whites, fresh: Separate eggs very carefully, leaving no trace of yolk, or they will not beat. Substitution: 3 tablespoons dried egg white plus ¼ cup cold water=3 fresh egg whites.

Firm ball: Caramel ball that feels somewhat firmer than a cold piece of regular caramel. Cooking temperature 244–246° F.

Fondant, creaming: Pour batch onto large baking sheet moistened lightly with cold water just before batch is poured on. DO NOT scrape out pot. Let cool until batch feels just warm, no longer hot. Scrape together in center of sheet, spread out over whole sheet; repeat, using long, firm strokes and holding spatula almost flat, until batch gets opaque and sets up, about 10–15 minutes, then knead smooth.

Gelatine, Knox unflavored: Substitution: any unflavored gelatine, preferably powdered. Do not heat over 150° F.

Gums and gumdrops: Impressions of plaster molds are made in trays of special molding starch, then hot gum syrup is cast into these impressions. Trays are then put into a 130° F. hot-room for 2–3 days. When gum centers are firm, they are removed from the starch trays and sugar-sanded. Because of the equipment involved, it would be almost impossible to make gumdrops or other gum confections at home.

Inversion: Sucrose (cane or beet sugar) solutions dry out and recrystallize in the air. Glucose and levulose (invert sugars) become wet by absorbing moisture from the air. Inversion means that part of the sucrose in a candy has inverted (changed) into glucose and levulose, preventing the candy from drying out or recrystallizing into a hard, grainy mass. Controlling recrystallization, and therefore softness, is achieved either by adding Karo syrup (dissolved invert sugars) to the candy, or by adding inversion agents, such as cream of tartar, citric acid, vinegar, or yeast, to invert some of the sucrose. Prolonged cooking of a sugar syrup at low heat will also cause inversion, but this is unsatisfactory, because the degree of inversion is hard to control, and also, the sugar will turn brown.

Jam, recooking: Put about ½ cup of strawberry or raspberry jam into a pot on low heat. Stir continuously. Cook 10–15 minutes, then cool by partially submerging pot in cold water and stirring. Removes excess moisture from jam to be used in crème centers.

Jelly beans: Impressions of center-shaped plaster molds are made in trays of special molding starch, then hot gum syrup is cast into the impressions. Trays are then put into a 130° F. hot-room for 2–3 days. The centers are then removed from the starch molds and covered with a smooth sugar coat in a revolving pan (dragée pan). When the coat is thick enough, the jelly beans are put into flat trays for drying. When they are dry enough, they are polished in revolving polishing pans. Each color and flavor has to go through this cycle separately, and it is evident that this is one confection that cannot be made at home.

Karo syrup: A clear, light (in color), medium-heavy syrup made from pure corn syrup (levulose and dextrose), with sugar, salt, and vanilla added. Better suited than pure corn syrup for candy recipes made at home, because Karo syrup flows easier and is easier to measure than the very heavy, pure corn syrup. However, if you wish to use pure corn syrup, use only about three-fourths of the amount given for Karo syrup and make up the difference with water. Use clear, white Karo syrup, rather than dark Karo syrup.

Lecithin: Resembles a dark, heavy syrup, is made from soya bean extract. Lecithin eases the surface tension of concoctions containing fat and helps prevent fat separation in highly cooked sugar syrups with a high butter or margarine content. Lecithin is contained in most margarine. It is also widely used in chocolate production, to make the chocolate more liquid for dipping or molding, and to add to the eating pleasure of the finished product, by helping it melt easier in your mouth.

Licorice, soft: Licorice is made from sugar, corn syrup, starch, flour, licorice extract, and color, cooked for a long time, pre-dried, and shaped with heavy extruders. Then the product has to go through a drying process again, before being cut and finished. Therefore, it would be next to impossible to make licorice at home.

Licorice flavor: Pure licorice extract is made from the tropical licorice root, is quite expensive, and is hardly obtainable in the retail trade. Therefore, we use anise oil in homemade candies, as a good substitute.

Low-calorie candies: Making this kind of confection is a rather tedious and complicated procedure, as the main building material of candies—sugar—has to be left out and replaced with edible cellulose, gum, or special chemical solutions, not obtainable in small quantities, and not obtainable at all from any retail store. The same is true of low-calorie chocolate, to be used for chocolate-coated pieces.

Marble slab: Used for creaming fondant and buttercrème. Moisten before pouring on batch, start creaming as soon as batch just feels warm, no longer hot.

Margarine: Made from hydrogenated vegetable oil. Interchangeable with butter, except in almond toffee, where the lecithin in the margarine is needed to keep the fat from separating from the rest of the batch. Not interchangeable with liquid cooking oils.

Medium ball: Caramel ball that feels fairly firm, but not hard, exactly as a finished piece of caramel should feel when cold. Cooking temperature 240–242° F.

Molasses: The natural byproduct of sugar refining. Use light molasses; to lighten up dark molasses: 1 part dark molasses plus 1 part Karo syrup=2 parts light molasses. Sulphured molasses, molasses bleached with sulphur dioxide, is interchangeable with unsulphured molasses. Note: batches containing molasses boil considerably higher than others.

Sanding: Place candy pieces on one half of a moist towel, fold other half of towel over candies to moisten them lightly all over.

Take the pieces out of the towel and roll them in granulated sugar.

Scoring: Press the greased edge of a knife or spatula on the surface of the candy batch to score it.

Set or set up: To become stiff, to harden, to change into a semi-solid or solid.

Soft ball: Caramel ball that feels somewhat softer than a regular piece of cold caramel. Cooking temperature 234–238° F.

Sugar, brown: Cane or beet sugar containing natural molasses, used to give a fine caramel or molasses flavor to confections. Use light or dark brown sugar, depending on your preference.

Sugar, confectioners' powdered: Sift before using.

Sugar, white: Cane and beet sugar are interchangeable.

Sugar crystals, adhering: Wash adhering sugar crystals down from the sides of the pot and the stirring paddle as soon as the batch has boiled up for the first time, using a small, clean brush dipped lightly in cold water. Don't use too much water for this. Or, cover the pot for 2–3 minutes, during which the resulting steam will dissolve the crystals.

Taffy, pulling: Form the precooled batch into a rope 2 inches thick. Pull until 2–3 feet long, fold, twist, pull again. Repeat for 6–8 minutes for *Pulled Molasses Taffy, Molasses Mint Taffy*, and *After-Dinner Mints*; 20 minutes for *Salt Water Taffy*.

Temperatures, cooking: Change according to thermometer test. Also, cooking a batch 2–3° F. higher than indicated will make it firmer and drier; 2–3° F. lower will make it softer.

Thermometer, testing: Check the thermometer in boiling water. It should read 212° F. If not, vary the cooking temperatures accordingly.

Yeast: Dry, powdered yeast or cake yeast are interchangeable. Dissolve into a liquid paste in warm water before adding. Destroyed by temperatures over 160° F.

Appendix A

SOME SOURCES FOR CANDY FLAVORINGS, COLORS, AND OTHER RAW MATERIALS

Agar-agar, dry, shredded, or in flakes: Obtainable in health stores or in drug stores.

Almond paste, pure: Sold mostly in cans of 7–8 pounds. Supply houses for bakeries and confectioners, also in some supermarkets, in smaller cans, and import stores.

Bonbon coating: This is not carried in any store yet, as it is used only for coating candies or cookies. Therefore, you will have to order it from a bakery or confectioner's supply house, or at your local candy store.

Candy flavors: The Shilling Company and the Crescent Company have a number of fine candy flavors on the shelves of groceries, supermarkets, department store food sections, and delicatessen stores, usually displayed with or near the spices. Import stores and larger drug stores may also carry candy flavors.

Chocolate coating, milk or bittersweet: Almost all supermarkets throughout the nation now carry large and small pieces of so-called break-up or block chocolate. Also most candy stores and the candy sections of department stores have pure chocolate coating on sale in any quantity you like. The most economical way, of course, is to purchase chocolate coating in standard 10-pound slabs, at the stores mentioned above. Sometimes, they may have to order 10-pound slabs for you specially from their suppliers, and it may be a few days or a week before you will get it, but you will find that everybody carrying chocolate coating in their stores will gladly oblige you, because 10 pounds of chocolate is a nice sale.

Citric acid, finely granulated: Your local drug store.

Coconut, finely shredded, plain or toasted: Most supermarkets carry plain, finely shredded, desiccated coconut in small packages. If the recipe calls for finely shredded toasted coconut, and you cannot obtain it at your local grocery store or confectioner's supply house, toast your own. See the Glossary. The same applies to finely shredded white coconut; you can grate fresh shelled coconut on a cheese grater and dry it in the oven. See the Glossary for instructions.

Decorettes, chocolate and colored: These "decorettes" are found in almost any supermarket in small transparent containers, in the cake decorating section. But for making candy batches of 1½ pounds or larger, one would have to buy at least a dozen of these containers to have enough decorettes to work with; and this is quite uneconomical. Here again, the best way is to buy or order them by the pound from your local candy store or the nearest bakery or confectioner's supply house.

Egg whites, dried: Bakery and confectionery supply houses, found in the Yellow Pages of the phone book.

Food colors, liquid: Liquid food colors are on display in most grocery stores, in the baking materials section. Liquid food colors can be used for coloring crèmes.

Food colors, paste: Paste colors are preferable for hard candies as well as for crèmes, because paste colors contain less water than liquid colors, and therefore there is less danger of making hard candies sticky or crèmes too soft. Most supply houses for bakeries or confectioners carry paste food colors in small jars. Consult the Yellow Pages in your phone book. There is such a supply house in every large city or town in the U.S.A. Also look for cake decoration supply houses.

Lecithin: Health stores.

Nut meats:

Raw, shelled Spanish peanuts: You can buy them in any

health store, or buy them in the shell at your local grocery and shell them yourself.

Brazil nuts: Bakery and confectioner's supply houses have them; also often on display in supermarkets, but buy only unsalted and unroasted Brazil nut meats, or buy them in the shells and shell them yourself.

Almonds, walnuts, pecans, filberts: If you cannot obtain these nuts raw, shelled, and unsalted at the grocery store or a health store, the best and most economical way is to buy these nuts in the shells and shell and chop them yourself.

Roasted and blanched almonds: Again, if you cannot obtain these nuts unsalted, roast and blanch them yourself. See the Glossary.

If you should still have difficulty locating a source of supply for any of the raw materials needed, you may order them through me. I will either take care of it myself, or will put you in touch with a supplier near you. Write to:

Martin K. Herrmann
P. O. Box ✗14152
Portland, Oregon 97214

Appendix B

SOME SOURCES FOR TOOLS, UTENSILS, AND OTHER MATERIALS FOR CANDY MAKING

Chocolate dipping fork and cherry dipping fork: Both dipping forks are made with a round handle, for easy turning between thumb and index finger, when flipping the chocolate-coated piece over before setting it down on the paper.

The chocolate dipping fork has two straight, parallel metal prongs, used for coating the piece with chocolate and then for decorating the coated piece with lines or dabs, or for dipping only, and then slipping the piece on the paper without decor, as is done with mint patties and other disk-shaped pieces.

The cherry dipping fork is also made of metal, has a loop on the end instead of prongs, and is used mainly for cordials or ball-shaped pieces, to manipulate and hold them more securely, in the loop, while dipping them in fondant or chocolate. The loop is also used to gather some additional chocolate for decorating the dipped pieces with a spiral or loop, not possible with a straight-pronged fork.

Mail-order houses for cake decorating utensils carry these dipping forks, usually imported from Europe. Addresses of these firms can be found in household and women's magazines, or in the Yellow Pages of the phone book. However, as there has been a constant demand for these dipping forks for the candy-making courses I have given, it was more practical and economical to have dipping forks made by a firm in Portland, according to my designs; and they have proved to be very practical and popular.

Crinkle-cups (paper cups): Some five-and-ten-cent stores and the stationery sections of department stores carry these small white or brown candy cups, especially around Christmas time. Also, any paper wholesale firm near you will give you the address of the nearest firm or store in your town selling candy cups.

Lollipop sticks: Many millions of these sticks, made of wood or rigid paper, are used the year round by a great number of candy firms throughout the country, and yet there are hardly any lollipop sticks sold in retail stores. But wooden meat skewers, easily obtained at your local butcher, make excellent lollipop sticks. You may also use toothpicks, but cut off the sharp points to prevent injuries to children.

Rubber mat, grooved: This is regular black rubber matting, with parallel grooves about ⅛ inch apart and about ⅛ inch deep, as used on floors or on stairs. Variety sections of department stores carry it, as do Sears, Roebuck and Company, Montgomery Ward, many five-and-ten-cent stores, and hardware and floor-covering stores. Buy it by the yard, as it comes, usually 36 inches wide. You will need only ⅓ yard, giving you a working surface of 12×36 inches. You may, of course, cut this piece into two 12×18-inch sections for easier handling.

Steel spatula, with a stiff blade: Paint stores, variety sections of supermarkets, or department stores. The edges of the blade of a new steel spatula are usually quite sharp. Round the edges slightly with emery cloth, or sandpaper, or on a grindstone, to prevent scratching your trays and baking sheets.

Thermometer: Taylor Candy-Jelly-Frosting thermometer. Variety sections of supermarkets, or larger drug stores or department stores.

If you cannot obtain dipping forks or other tools from the above-mentioned sources, feel free to write to me for further information:

Martin K. Herrmann
P. O. Box ⚡14152
Portland, Oregon 97214

Index

After-dinner mints, 36–37
Agar-agar
  defined, 154
  sources for, 161
Agar-agar jellies, 107–11
Alcoholic fruit cordials, 143–50
Almond (base) paste, 101, 154–55
  sources for, 161
Almonds
  blanching, 154
  in caramel popcorn, 127–28
  chocolate bark with, 60
  chocolate caramel with, 45
  in fudge (see Fudge)
  roasting, 154
  sources for, 163
Almond toffee, 122–25
America
  consumption of candy in U.S., 19
  and history of candy, 18
Apothecaries, 18
Apple-cinnamon jellies, 114
Apple-nut jellies, 113
Applesauce jellies, 112–17

Baking sheets and pans, 22
Baking soda, defined, 154

Base (almond) paste, 101, 154–55
  sources for, 161
Batch, defined, 155
Bonbon coating, 58, 155
  sources for, 161
Brazil brittle, 41
Brazil nuts
  penuche with, 93
  sources for, 163
Butter, 155
Buttercrème, 84–93
  basic, 84–86
  buttermint centers, 88–89
  centers, 86–90
  chocolate centers, 87–88
  chocolate fudge, 92
  chocolate-mint centers, 88
  maple-walnut centers, 90
  opera crèmes, 89
  penuche fudge, 92–93
  rum-nut centers, 87
  vanilla fudge, 90–91
Buttered caramel popcorn, 127–29
Buttermint crème centers, 88–89
Butterscotch drops, 29

Candied fruit peel, 138–40
Caramel, 42–47

chocolate-nut, 45
cutting, 44–45, 155
milk, 42–45
milk, for pecan rolls, 135–36
popcorn, 127–29
testing, 43–44, 155
turtles, 46–48
Cashew brittle, 40
Cherries, for cordials, 145
Cherry crèmes, 96
Cherry dipping fork, 164
Chocolate
coatings, 48–58
sources for, 161–62
decorating of chocolates, 56–57
dipping in, 51–55, 155–56 (see also Cordials; Jellies; Marzipan; Nuts; Toffee)
buttercrème centers for, 86–90
fork for, 52ff., 164
hand-rolled crème centers for, 75–79
in history of candy making, 18ff.
melting of, 49–50, 156
tempering of, 50–52, 156
unsweetened, 155
See also Pralines; Rocky Road; Truffles; specific chocolate-coated candies
Chocolate bark, 59–60
Chocolate caramel, nut-, 45
Chocolate clusters, 59, 60
Chocolate coconut mounds, 132
Chocolate crème centers, 87–88
mint, 88

Chocolate fudge, 92
Chocolate nougat, 121–22
Chocolate white-dots, 98
Cinnamon-apple jellies, 114
Cinnamon drops, 30
Citric acid, 25, 156
sources for, 162
Cocoa, 18
Coconut
shredding, 156
sources for, 162
toasting, 156
Coconut balls, 97
Coconut brittle, 40
Coconut crème centers, 80
Coconut mounds, 132–33
Coffee doughnuts, 95–96
Coffee-walnut marzipan, 102
Cold water, use of, 23
"Conditors," 19
Confectioners, 18–19
Consistency, 24
Cordialize, defined, 156
Cordials, 143–53
alcoholic, 143–50
non-alcoholic, 150–53
Cortez, Hernando, 18
Crèmes
quick, 96–97
See also Buttercrème; Fondant
Crinkle-cups, 165

Decorettes, sources for, 162
Dipping forks, 52ff., 164
Divinity, 126–27
Dragées, 156
Drops, hard candy, how to form, 25–26

Egg whites, dried, 157
  sources for, 162
Egg whites, fresh, 157
Europe, and candy history, 18–19

Filbert brittle, 41
Filberts
  for praline, 140–42
  sources for, 163
Firm ball, defined, 157
Flavors, sources for, 161
Fondant, 70–83, 157
  basic sugar crème, 70–75
  coconut centers, 80
  crème centers, 75–80
  fruit crème centers, 78–80
  fruit crème patties, 81–83
  lemon centers, 79
  lemon patties, 83
  mint centers, 78–79
  mint patties, 82–83
  orange centers, 79
  orange patties, 83
  raspberry centers, 80
  raspberry patties, 83
  strawberry centers, 80
  summer crème patties, 81–83
  See also Cordials; Specialties
Food colors, sources for, 162
French whipped-cream truffles, 129–31
Fruit crème centers, 78–80
Fruit crème patties, summer, 81–83
Fruit jellies, agar-agar, 107–11
Fruit jellies, gelatine and apple-sauce, 112–17
Fruit peel, candied, 138–40
Fudge, 90–93

chocolate, 92
penuche, 92–93
vanilla, 90

Gelatine, 157
Gelatine and applesauce jellies, 112–17
Germany, 17
Gingerbread, 17, 19
Glossary, 154–60
Grapefruit peel, candied, 138–40
Grape jellies, 110
Gums and gumdrops, 157

Hard candies, 25–41
  Brazil brittle, 41
  butterscotch drops, 29
  cashew brittle, 40
  cinnamon drops, 30
  coconut brittle, 40
  filbert brittle, 41
  general procedure for, 25–29
  lemon squares, 30
  licorice drops, 31
  lollipops, 31
    sticks for, 165
  mint drops or bars, 29
  mints, after-dinner, 36–37
  mint taffy, molasses, 36
  molasses taffy, 32–35
    mint, 36
  peanut brittle, 37–40
  raspberry squares, 30–31
  strawberry squares, 30–31
History of candy making, 17–19
Honey, 18
Honey nougat, 118–21
  chocolate, 121–22

Indians, 18
Inversion, 157–58

Jam, recooking, 158
Jellies, agar-agar, 107–11
  basic batch, 107–8
  chocolate-coated, 109
  grape, 110
  lemon, 110
  mint, 109
  Neapolitan, 108–9
  orange, 111
  raspberry, 111
  strawberry, 110
  sugar-sanded, 109
Jellies, gelatine and applesauce,
    112–17
  basic, 112–13
  chocolate-covered, 113
  cinnamon-apple, 114
  lemon, 114
  mint, 114
  mint, green and white, 115–16
  nut-apple, 113
  orange, 115
  raspberry, 115
  raspberry, red and white, 116–
    17
  sandwich, green and white,
    115–16
  sandwich, red and white, 116–
    17
  strawberry, 117
  strawberry, red and white, 116–
    17
  sugar-sanded, 113
Jelly beans, 158

Karo syrup, 158

Lecithin, 158
  sources for, 162
Lemon crème centers, 79
Lemon crème patties, summer, 83
Lemon jellies (agar-agar), 110
Lemon jellies (applesauce), 114
Lemon peel, candied, 138–40
Lemon squares, 30
Licorice
  flavor, 159
  soft, 158–59
Licorice drops, 31
Lollipops, 31
  sticks for, 165
Low-calorie candies, 159

Maple-walnut crème centers, 90
Marble slabs, 73, 85–86, 159
Margarine, 159
Marshmallow, 62–69
  rocky road, 66–69
  toasted, 62–65
Marzipan, 101–6
  chocolate-coated, 101–2
  coffee-walnut, 102
  confections, 103–5
  potatoes, 105–6
  rum, 102
  toasting and glazing of, 104–5
  vanilla, 102
Medium ball, defined, 159
Milk caramel, 42–45
  for pecan rolls, 135–36
Mint centers
  buttercrème, 88–89
  chocolate, 88
  fondant, 78–79
Mint drops or bars, 29

Mint jellies (agar-agar), 109
Mint jellies (applesauce), 114
    green and white, 115–16
Mint patties
    quick, 98
    summer, 82–83
Mints, after-dinner, 36–37
Mints, thin-
    crème centers for, 78
    dipping, 57
Molasses, 159
Molasses taffy, 32–35
    mint, 36
Monasteries, 18
Montezuma, 18

Neapolitan jellies, 108–9
Neapolitans, 99–100
Non-alcoholic cordials, 150–53
Nougat, honey, 118–21
    chocolate, 121–22
Nut-apple jellies, 113
Nut brittles, 37–41
    Brazil, 41
    cashew, 40
    coconut, 40
    filbert, 41
    peanut, 37–40
Nut caramel, chocolate-, 45
Nut clusters, chocolate, 59, 60
Nut-rum crème centers, 87
Nuts
    chocolate bark with, 59, 60
    chocolate-dipped, 59, 61
    fudge with (see Fudge)
    sources for, 162–63
    See also Almonds; Walnuts
Nutty goody, 98

Opera crèmes, 89
    quick, 96–97
Orange crème centers, 79
Orange crème patties, summer, 83
Orange jellies (agar-agar), 111
Orange jellies (applesauce), 115
Orange peel, candied, 138–40

Peaches, for cordials, 145
Peanut brittle, 37–40
Peanut butter squares, 97
Peanuts, sources for, 162–63
Pecan rolls, 135–38
Pecans
    in caramel popcorn, 127–28
    sources for, 163
Penuche fudge, 92–93
Peter, Daniel, 19
Pineapple, for cordials, 145
Popcorn, caramel, 127–29
Pots, 22
Praline, 140–42
Pulled molasses taffy, 32–35
Pulling of candies, 160. See also
    Pulled Molasses Taffy

Quantities, 22–23
Quickie candies, 94–100
    basic batch, 94–95
    cherry crèmes, 96
    chocolate white-dots, 98
    coconut balls, 97
    coffee doughnuts, 95–96
    mint patties, 98
    Neapolitans, 99–100
    nutty goody, 98
    opera crèmes, 96–97
    peanut butter squares, 97
    rum-walnut candies, 95

Raspberry crème centers, 80
Raspberry crème patties, summer,
83
Raspberry jellies (agar-agar), 111
Raspberry jellies (applesauce),
115
red and white, 116–17
Raspberry squares, 30–31
Raw materials, 20
sources for, 161–63
Rocky road, 66–69
Rome, 18
Rubber mat, grooved, 165
Rum marzipan, 102
Rum-nut crème centers, 87
Rum-walnut candies, 95

Salt-water taffy, 133–35
Sanded jellies, 109, 113
"Sanding," 28–29, 159–60
Sandwich jelly
green and white, 115–16
red and white, 116–17
Scoring, defined, 160
"Seeding" of chocolate, 50–51
"Set," or "set up," defined, 160
Soft ball, defined, 160
Spaniards, 18
Spatulas, 165
Specialties, 118
almond toffee, 122–25
buttered caramel popcorn, 127–
29
candied fruit peel, 138–40
chocolate nougat, 121–22
coconut mounds, 132–33
divinity, 126–27
French whipped-cream truffles,
129–31

pecan rolls, 135–38
praline, 140–42
salt-water taffy, 133–35
tender honey nougat, 118–21
Square hard candies, how to form,
26–28
Strawberries, for cordials, 145
Strawberry coconut mounds, 132
Strawberry crème centers, 80
Strawberry jellies (agar-agar), 110
Strawberry jellies (applesauce),
117
red and white, 116–17
Strawberry squares, 30–31
Sugar, 18, 160
boiling, 23–24, 160
invert, 157–58
kinds, defined, 160
Sugar-coating. See "Sanding"
Sugar crème, basic, 70–75
Sugar-sanded jellies (agar-agar),
109
Sugar-sanded jellies (applesauce),
113
Summer crème patties, 81–83
lemon, 83
mint, 82–83
orange, 83
raspberry, 83
"Sweets," 17, 18, 19

Taffy, 160
molasses, 32–35
molasses mint, 36
salt-water, 133–35
Taylor thermometer, 21, 165
Temperatures, 22, 160
Tender honey nougat, 118–21
Thermometers, 21, 22ff., 160, 165

Toasted marshmallow, 62–65
Toffee, almond, 122–25
Tools and utensils, 21
    sources for, 164–65
Truffles, French whipped-cream,
    129–31
Turtles, 46–48

Utensils, 21
    sources for, 164–65

Vanilla coconut mounds, 132
Vanilla fudge, 90–91
Vanilla marzipan, 102

Walnut-apple jellies, 113

Walnut caramel, chocolate-, 45
Walnut-coffee marzipan, 102
Walnut crème centers, maple-, 90
Walnut crème centers, rum-, 87
Walnut divinity, 126–27
Walnut-rum candies, 95
Walnuts
    fudge with (see Fudge)
    rocky road with, 66–69
    sources for, 163
Weight, 23
Whipped-cream truffles, French,
    129–31
Wrapping of candies, 28

Yeast, 160